# Worship

SIMPLICITY & INTIMACY WITH JESUS

## JEFF KINLEY

Copyright © 2017 by Jeff Kinley

All rights reserved.

No part of this publication may be reproduced, stored in a retrieval system or transmitted in any way by any means, electronic, mechanical, photocopy, recording or otherwise without the prior permission of the author except as provided by USA copyright law.

Scripture quotations taken from the New American Standard Bible® (NASB), Copyright © 1960, 1962, 1963, 1968, 1971, 1972, 1973, 1975, 1977, 1995 by The Lockman Foundation Used by permission. www.Lockman.org

**Worship**
Simplicity & Intimacy with Jesus

Cover design by Jeff Kinley
Interior Page design by True Potential, Inc.

ISBN: 978-1-943852-45-1 (paperback)
ISBN: 978-1-943852-46-8 (ebook)
Library of Congress Control Number: 2017935009

True Potential, Inc
PO Box 904, Travelers Rest, SC 29690
www.truepotentialmedia.com

Printed in the United States of America.

*To Hadley*

# Contents

Introduction ........................................................................................9

**Chapter 1** ........................................................................................ 11
Hardwired for Worship
 "No-Brainers" ............................................................................11
 Garden-Variety Couple ..............................................................12
 Food Poisoning ..........................................................................15
 The Wonderful World of Sin .....................................................20

**Chapter 2** ........................................................................................ 22
The Cover Up
 System Failure ............................................................................24
 Who's Seeking Whom? ...............................................................26
 Fatal Fallout ................................................................................31
 Losing the Leaves .......................................................................35
 Ready to lose those leaves? .........................................................36

**Chapter 3** ........................................................................................ 38
Audience of One
The Object/Focus of Worship
 Many Faiths, One God? .............................................................38
 Sin at Sinai .................................................................................39
 It Truly is about "Who You Know" ...........................................44

**Chapter 4** ........................................................................................ 47
The Great I AM
The Grandeur of Worship
 "I AM THE GREATEST" ..........................................................47
 "I Am Great in Creation" ...........................................................48
 "I Am Great in Wisdom" ...........................................................50
  (Isaiah 40:13–14)
 "I Am Great in Sovereignty" ......................................................52
  (Isaiah 40:15, 17, 21–25)
 100% Chance of Reign ...............................................................59
 "I Am Great in Righteousness" ..................................................62
  (Isaiah 40:16)

## Chapter 5 .................................................................. 64
The Grace Factor
Motivation for Worship

"Cheap Grace" ....................................................................................64

I Once Was Lost..................................................................................66

I Kissed Legalism Goodbye ................................................................68

Myth #1 ..............................................................................................69
>   Obeying God's Rules Can Save Me
>   (Galatians 1:6–9; 3:24; 5:1–4)

Myth #2 ..............................................................................................72
>   After Salvation, Obeying God's Rules Improves My Standing Before God
>   (Galatians 3:24–26)

Myth #3 ..............................................................................................74
>   Living by the Rules is the Best Way for Me to Mature in Christ

Ten Deadly Effects of Being a Legalistic "Rule-Keeper" .........................75

Myth #4 ..............................................................................................79
>   Under Grace, I Can Now Sin All I Want
>   (Galatians 5:13)

Peter....................................................................................................80

Paul.....................................................................................................80

James...................................................................................................80

"All This For You"...............................................................................81

## Chapter 6 .................................................................. 84
Dancing on the Edge
Extreme Worship

The Outer Limits ................................................................................84

Boxers or Briefs?..................................................................................85

A Party for Doctor Jesus .....................................................................87

Desperately Devoted ...........................................................................93

## Chapter 7 ................................................................ 103
When Little is Much
Sacrificial Worship

Stayin' Alive......................................................................................103

"Mitey" Sacrifice...............................................................................104

"Dad, I don't want it back."..............................................................106

Miracle on a Mountainside...............................................................108

Contents    7

**Chapter 8** .................................................................................. **115**
Unplugged
Simple Worship
    There's Something About Mary ............................................................118
    Dead Man Walking ...............................................................................123
    The Smell of Worship ............................................................................127
    Recapturing Your Worship ....................................................................131

**Chapter 9** .................................................................................. **133**
It Was a God Thing
Unexplainable Worship
    Scene One: Angels Watching Over Us ..................................................137
    Scene Two: Rebel Forces Go South .......................................................138
    Scene Three: Will the Real God Please Show Up? ................................140

**Chapter 10** ................................................................................ **145**
When Your World is Falling Apart
    So What's the "Benefit Package?" .........................................................153

**Chapter 11** ................................................................................ **157**
Royal Want Ads
God is Seeking Worshipers
    The "Seeker-Sensitive" God? .................................................................157
    Wonderful Stranger ...............................................................................158
    #awkward .............................................................................................160
    A True Worshiper's Heartbeat ...............................................................164
    The Integrity of Worship ......................................................................165
    You with me? ........................................................................................169
        Worship that is Rare and Well-Done
    Guess Who? ..........................................................................................171
    Well, WELL! ........................................................................................173

Endnotes ..................................................................................... 176

# Introduction

Worship.

The mere mention of the word conjures up images and emotions uniquely interwoven into our Christian faith. But have you ever really wondered what the word actually *means*? What does worship look like? How can we ever know if we're *doing it* right, according to God's Word? Or if we're even doing it at all? At times the idea of worship may seem very limited, boxed in by a narrowly-defined, confusing array of practices, preferences, and traditions scattered all across the Christian landscape. Practices we dare not disassociate from a Sunday morning experience. Worship often seems to be both everywhere and nowhere all at once. Worship songs. Worship bands. Worship leaders. Worship conferences. And tagging along come the concert venues, stage lighting, choreographed dances and hand raisings, and verbal or musical worship prompts meant to jump-start sleepy or apathetic congregations or audiences. But despite these all too familiar visuals, if you try to define this concept, you're likely to end up with a rambling, ethereal explanation that hovers somewhere between heaven and earth, but consistently connecting with neither. What we're left with is a sort of sentimental, mystical feeling inside, the kind we only get when we "worship."

But rather than attempt to explain it merely from our limited, mortal experiences, why not look at what God says on the subject in His Word. Sounds good, right? But in doing this, we eventually discover there is no chapter and verse definitively articulating the what, when, how, where, and why of worship. Rather, what God, through the Bible, gives us is the big picture of worship—from Genesis to Revelation. And fortunately, from surveying this scriptural panorama of praise, a portrait slowly unveils itself. From this journey through God's only authoritative record of truth, we gain not only wisdom and understanding, but also the heart motivation to become what we were originally created to be…worshipers.

In this book, together we'll debunk false notions of worship, replacing them with divine truth straight from the heart of God. We'll cast aside man-made perceptions and cultural practices that have colored and skewed our understanding of what it means to be worshipful. Through renewing our minds, we'll reboot, embracing a fresh experience with worship, leading us into the very simplicity and intimacy with Jesus Christ for which we long. Chances are, you're reading this because you have an interest in the subject. If so, read on and prepare yourself to encounter the glorious adventure for which you were made.

Jeff Kinley

CHAPTER 1

# Hardwired for Worship

> We are here to be worshippers first, and workers second.
> – A.W. Tozer

## "No-Brainers"

Some things in life take great effort to learn and perfect. These are the activities, skills and disciplines that just don't come easy for most of us. They require effort, exercise and sometimes even excruciating practice. They test our patience and sometimes even our sanity. Try as we might, these activities seem to exist in a realm just beyond the reach of our fingertips. We just can't quite "succeed" at them. And even more disheartening is seeing those individuals who appear effortlessly to master difficult things with great ease. These people can be positively annoying because, for some reason, what is complex and difficult for most is simple and second nature for them. We struggle for years to be proficient at activities and skills that are a "breeze" for them. You know, things like: Calculus, ice-skating, playing the piano, riding a horse, writing HTML code, dunking a basketball, debugging a computer, cooking, speaking a foreign language, reading music, understanding the stock market, skiing moguls in 24-inch snow powder, sailing a boat, solving a riddle or crossword puzzle, fixing a car or drawing a picture.

What about you? Which things, while attempting to learn or master, have instead sent you into emotional orbit? Well, don't be discouraged or freak out about it. Everyone has his or her own strengths and skills. And yours are as unique as anyone else's. Everybody has something that comes naturally to him or her. These raw talents are so habitual and routine that they require virtually no effort whatsoever. They're the "no-brainers" in life that appear to run via some "autopilot" system hidden deep within our psyche. We don't plan or program them. They just happen...all by themselves. We don't have to work at them or practice them since they seem virtually instinctive.

Truth is our lives are filled with movements, motions and mannerisms that occur without any conscious prompting whatsoever. Things like breathing, blinking, swallowing, thinking, dreaming, speaking, watching, listening, singing, resting, playing, loving, learning, living…and worshiping.

> Worshiping is a natural, unlearned activity that all people do.

Worshiping is a natural, unlearned activity that all people do. Not just religious people, and not just Christians. Worshiping is something every one of us does, and it's just as real, regular, and as unconsciously done as breathing. Like inhaling and exhaling, worshiping is what we human beings effortlessly and naturally do every day. In fact, it may be the most common and consistent habit we practice. But how can this be? And why?

## **Garden-Variety Couple**

If you can, scroll to the "menu" section in your biblical memory file marked "Genesis." Now choose "Adam and Eve." Remember them? This first-ever couple was made as the prototype of the human race that would follow them. Of course we all know Adam and his beautiful bride, Eve, were made "in the image of God" (Genesis 1:26–27). And as a part of that image, they (and we) were given the awesome ability to think and reason on a level far above the animal kingdom. As such, humanity remains the ultimate crown of God's great creation. But we also enjoy a privilege even greater than this—something more unique, honorable, and beneficial. Inherent within the image of God in us is the awesome capacity for *relationship*—specifically, relationship with *God*.

For Adam and Eve, their relationship with God mirrored their relationship with their environment and with each other—perfect and complete, lacking in nothing. They were *made* to worship God and walk with Him. Intricately designed to do life with Him. For them, finding paradise didn't involve a flight to Maui. They didn't dream of a better life. They lived that dream 24/7. It was their own little version of heaven on earth, and they had it all—right there in the Garden called "Eden" (Genesis 1:26–2:25). In the fullest sense of the word, they were *complete*.

Life was good.

However, just a short time earlier, life hadn't been so good for Adam. It was during his "B.E." (or "Before Eve") period. God and Adam both recognized that the man needed a human companion—a counterpart and soul mate. So the Lord did something about it.

Genesis 2:18 records, "Then the LORD God said, 'It is not good for the man to be alone; I will make him a helper suitable for him.'"

So He made Eve. And she, no doubt, was the ultimate woman. Not only did she possess all the necessary physical characteristics of history's first prototypical woman, but she was also the total package *inside* as well. Her personality, temperament, intelligence and emotional makeup were, well . . . perfect. Body, brains and balanced emotions. Every godly man's ideal woman. And fortunately for Adam, his dream woman came to life right before his very eyes. Eve was "tailor-made" for her man. Scripture says it happened like this:

> "And the LORD God fashioned into a woman the rib which He had taken from the man, and brought her to the man. And the man said, 'This is now bone of my bones, and flesh of my flesh; She shall be called Woman, because she was taken out of Man.'" (Genesis 2:23)

We can only guess at Adam's level of excitement and gratitude upon receiving his newly fashioned female gift from God. Scripture doesn't fill in all the blanks for us, and it would be unfair to read too much between the lines here. However, we do know that Adam responded with an acknowledgment that not only honored her, but also demonstrated his leadership in naming her.[1] As the head and original representative of the human race, that was the job tasked to him. But I think we can safely say that having recognized his need for companionship, he was very, very excited to see her.

Adam was the pinnacle of perfection as well—a God-made man who perhaps sported a chiseled physique to match his rugged but gentlemanly charm. And Eve instantly responded to the one for whom she was made. Her man was also the total package, inside and out. His leadership was filled with care and honor for his woman. And together they would live and love each other, beginning their journey with God in their paradise home (Genesis 1:19–31).

Here was a pair literally "made for each other." It was the first match "made in Heaven." And as such, they were complete, lacking in absolutely nothing. But wait, it gets even better.

They were also *unashamed*.

The Bible explains:

"For this cause a man shall leave his father and his mother, and shall cleave to his wife; and they shall become one flesh. And the man and his wife were both naked and were not ashamed." (Genesis 2:24–25)

Adam and Eve were created "au natural." In the proverbial "buff." And even after their creation, they remained in their unclothed state. Clothing was not needed in a perfect environment where the temperature was just right at all times. And nothing in creation threatened their bodies. No thorns, poison ivy or sunburn.[2] So there was no need for such things as "clothes" yet. However, beyond this, their external nakedness was something intended by God to picture the inward intimacy the couple shared with each other. They had no guilt regarding their nakedness because no sin or shame was associated with it. Eve was married to Adam from the moment she was created, and God's design for them was that they enjoy ultimate intimacy on every level – spiritually, emotionally, intellectually, socially, and sexually.

As co-regents with God, they also exercised dominion over the animal kingdom, including the fish of the sea and the birds of the air (Genesis 1:28; Psalm 8:6–8).

There weren't a whole lot of rules in the Garden. Noticeably absent were commands the Lord would later give His people, namely *"You shall worship the Lord your God only"* (Deuteronomy 6:13). Clearly, God had no need to tell them to do what came so naturally for them. Their ability to love God was virtually unlimited. They honored Him without any prompting whatsoever. I have a hard time imagining what that must have been like. They needed no reminders. No spiritual wake up calls. No necessary prodding or accountability. They simply chose to worship their God because it was their *default mode*. They were rightly related to each other and to Him. Things were very good in the Garden, and the forecast looked great for the human race. What more could a man, woman or couple possibly want? Here was a man and a woman with no problems, stress, conflict, confusion or drama. They were totally fulfilled. Nothing could possibly go wrong, right?

Wrong.

## Food Poisoning

Unfortunately, something went wrong. Adam and Eve lost it all. Everything. They went bust. The bottom fell out, and their world came crashing down on top of them. But how? How could anyone possibly screw up a situation as great as theirs? What were they thinking? Obviously, our first parents didn't plan it that way. Who would? They didn't set out to ruin their lives. But in doing so, they indelibly marked

> They had no guilt regarding their nakedness because no sin or shame was associated with it.

*ours*. Quite the contrary, it happened like most of our failures do—subtly and in a seemingly harmless manner. They made their first mistake when they listened to a voice other than God's.

> Now the serpent was more crafty than any of the wild animals the LORD God had made. He said to the woman, "Did God really say, 'You must not eat from any tree in the garden'?" (Genesis 3:1)

Wait a second. Where did this serpent come from? And how did he manage to slither in and write himself into this beautiful creation narrative? Here's the backstory:

Long before he spoke through false prophets and "angels of light," Satan spoke through a snake.[3] Having been ejected from Heaven, the angel formerly known as "Lucifer" was cast down to earth following a failed coup attempt.[4] It is not known how long Satan was on earth before he initiated his temptation of Adam and Eve. The timing between his fall from Heaven and his appearance in the Garden is information not revealed to us in Scripture. We do know that angels were created before the earth was made and that Satan was expelled from Heaven prior to launching his deceptive attack on Adam and his wife.[5]

Previous to their encounter with the serpent, Adam and Eve recognized and respected one voice only—God's. His voice was immediately known and acknowledged. His words needed no clarification or explanation. When God spoke to humanity's parents, He connected with their minds and spirits. His message was received, remembered and obeyed. That is, up until a snake opened his own mouth.

Now, for the first time, they listened to another's words. And though it was the wrong voice, it didn't seem eerie or evil to them. Had this been the case, they wouldn't have been so persuaded by it. On the contrary, the serpent's voice was soothing and conversational. Interestingly, there's no indication Eve was surprised to hear a reptile speak to her. Was this simply one more miraculous element God had encoded into His masterfully crafted creation?

Whatever her initial thoughts upon hearing the snake's voice were, it marked the first time Adam and Eve opened themselves to alternative ideas about God, life and truth. This historic moment began what rapidly became a downward spiraling experience. It was one fatal mistake that opened the door to a whole series of unfortunate human events. And it began when Adam and Eve were *persuaded to believe a lie about God.*

> The woman said to the serpent, "We may eat fruit from the trees in the garden, but God did say, 'You must not eat fruit from the tree that is in the middle of the garden, and you must not touch it, or you will die.'" "You will not surely die," the serpent said to the woman. "For God knows that when you eat of it your eyes will be opened, and you will be like God, knowing good and evil." (Genesis 3:2–5) When the woman saw that the fruit of the tree was good for food and pleasing to the eye, and also desirable

for gaining wisdom, she took some and ate it. She also gave some to her husband, who was with her, and he ate it. (Genesis 3:6)

Commonly believed to be the former preeminent worship leader in Heaven, Satan was expelled after leading an unsuccessful rebellion against God and His throne (Ezekiel 28:14; Isaiah 14:12–14). Because of this, he became bitterly opposed to God and those who bore His image. The first created humans were a lingering reminder to Satan of the God who thwarted his attempted ascension to glory. Perhaps seeing that glory displayed in creation brought to mind his former heavenly prestige, position, and all he had forfeited by his failed overthrow against the Creator. The couple was a walking audio-visual reminder to Satan, and their presence in Paradise personified his punishment.

And he hated them for it.

And so, discerning their innocence, he seized upon the opportunity to exact his revenge on Yahweh. Possessing the reptilian body, the devil manifested himself via the vocal cords of the serpent, now snake.[6] As a superior intellectual being, this Satan-filled serpent surely communicated as much with voice inflection as he did with the words themselves. Scripture doesn't tell us the size of this reptile, but it is very likely he spoke to Eve while on the ground rather than from a tree branch, as is traditionally depicted.[7]

And so, Lucifer calmly whispers his sinful sales pitch to the unsuspecting newlyweds.

> "You know, the three of us, we have a lot in common. This God you obey, I too have worshiped. In fact, I have known Him a long, long time. Longer than you. And I am well acquainted with all His ways. Indeed, I was a part of a very select few who got to see Him up close and personal. And because of my easy access to Him, I was privileged to know things about Him that none of the other created ones knew.
>
> But I must tell you how disappointed I soon became because what I learned both shocked and disturbed me. Imagine my surprise at discovering that instead of being the "good God" He professes to be, He is in fact a deceptive deity. You see, God teases you by saying you can 'look, but not touch.' Then He says

you can 'touch, but not taste. Taste, but not swallow. Swallow, but not enjoy!'

Sadly, I discovered He really isn't so good after all. It's all just a bunch of hype and threats to keep you under His control. He doesn't want you to know what He knows, because by knowing, you then become His equal. He's hogging all that 'godness' for Himself. In reality, He's insecure and selfish. And He's holding out on you, too. There is so much more to life than what He offers. There is real living outside this Garden Planet. Trust me, I know. I've been on the outside, and it's great.

As a result, I now have worshipers just like He does. I mean, why wouldn't you want to be a god? Why not experience something far better than being a servant. You can be worshiped, too!

Of course, I'm only telling you these things because I just don't want to see you get hurt by Him like I was. Somebody has to blow the whistle here and tell the truth. But don't take my word for it. Go ahead. See for yourself. Take and eat. This God of yours, trust me…He isn't worth worshiping."

Moses puts the conversation in more succinct, inspired language. But that's the spirit behind the serpent's words. And, apparently, it all sounded fairly convincing to Eve and her hubby, so much so that they bought into the lie and signed on the bottom line. But in doing so, they made a much bigger mistake than buying non-existent land in the Everglades. Their fatal faux pas was choosing to believe that fulfillment awaited them outside of God's provision. They embraced this new and unusual idea that there actually was something *better* than being a worshiper of the true God. And so, with human history hinging on this one single moment, all of creation held its breath.

And they ate.

When the woman saw that the fruit of the tree was good for food and pleasing to the eye, and also desirable for gaining wisdom, she took some and ate it. She also gave some to her husband, who was with her, and he ate it. (Genesis 3:6)

Amazingly, however, nothing immediately happened to the honeymoon couple. No lightning bolts from the sky. No sharp pain in their stomachs. No Montezuma's Revenge. No alarms or sirens going off in the Garden. No armed guards rushing in to arrest them. No devil horns sprouting from their heads. In fact, just the opposite occurred. Their initial sensation was the sweet and satisfying taste of this "fruit," like the first bite of a juicy apple or what you feel when sinking your teeth into a delicious cheeseburger. It, no doubt, felt amazing. Moist. Succulent. Rich. Ripe. Pleasing to the eyes *and* to the taste buds. This fruit was enjoyable. And pleasurable. It felt good in the mouth.

In short, Adam and his bride discovered what Scripture later affirms—sin is often *very* fun![8] Let's not deny it. Too often we downplay the pleasure associated with sin. But without it, none of us would ever give in to temptation! That's because sin and temptation involve things that are appealing. We are lured away from God by experiences that promise to be refreshing, not repugnant. For why would we commit the same sin again and again unless it brought us some sort of personal satisfaction. From the feeling of superiority we enjoy when we put another person down to the drug-like sensation of immoral sex, sin almost always tastes good with the first bite.

> Too often we downplay the pleasure associated with sin. But without it, none of us would ever give in to temptation!

But for Adam and Eve, though that forbidden fruit did indeed taste great, it turned out to be less filling. Since their formation, these humans had worshiped and pursued only their Creator. Yet now, the storyline takes a wicked twist. They had come upon a hairpin turn, and instead of slowing down to navigate it, they pressed the pedal and floored it, running straight through God's guardrail and over the cliff. Against all logic and sound judgment, they trusted a creature instead of the Creator. They bowed down to an altar of self in a momentary act of spiritual insanity. And just for a brief moment, it felt so good. So *right*.

## The Wonderful World of Sin

Unexpectedly, sin's narcotic *buzz* left them almost as quickly as it had come, with their hangover kicking in before the party was even over. And when it did, they began crashing hard and fast. They had taken the bait; the hook was set deep in them, and Satan had reeled them in.

Scripture records, "Then the eyes of both of them were opened, and they realized they were naked." (Genesis 3:7)

The serpent was right after all. Their eyes were opened, and they did indeed become enlightened. But at the same time, their souls were darkened. In an instant, they passed through an unseen portal leading to another world. It was a world their virgin minds could not possibly have previously imagined. And the consequences of their single act of disobedience swept over them like a nauseating tidal wave of regret.

And that was only the beginning of sin's shock wave.

The man and woman were beginning to realize the now popular maxim: *"Sin will take you farther than you want to go, keep you longer than you want to stay and cost you pay more than you want to pay."*

Adam and Eve over-drafted their spiritual bank account. Their choice set in motion a long-lasting avalanche of both damaging and damning consequences. And the aftershocks brought experiences they had never known before. Things like shame, guilt, grief, pain, sadness, loneliness, loss… and confusion. Added to this list was a hollow emptiness, which now echoed in their souls. That relationship with God was interrupted by sin. Disconnected by a previous intimacy with the Father, their experience with Him turned barren and distant. A darkness came over them. Their spiritual vitality was now silent. Lifeless. They had allowed history's most notorious thief to plunder their heart-home.

This horrible sin of self-worship changed every conceivable part of their person, influencing every function of their humanity.

*Spiritually*, they instantly died, afterward only able to produce offspring of like nature. Their children would now be born dead in spirit.[9] In fact, it's entirely possible that Satan's plan to corrupt humanity was implemented soon after creation to prevent this innocent couple from reproducing and populating the earth with pure worshipers of God. And it took only one birth to demonstrate how this deceiving drug of self-worship they had ingested would cause fatal flashbacks for the rest of human history.

But spiritual death wasn't the only outcome of their action. Like a deadly virus, sin also affected their *minds*. As a result, their thoughts would no longer naturally turn to God. Instead, a concerted effort was required in order to think about things that are spiritual, godly, and right. Actually, sin caused a type of "brain damage." Adam and Eve lost part of their mental capacities that day in the Garden. Parasitic lies and self-generated deception would now find a welcoming home in the human mind.[10]

Sin also altered their *emotions*. Formerly strong, balanced and harmonious, they became weak, volatile and unstable. From this point on, humankind would battle a roller coaster emotional experience from day to day, with relationships suffering because of it. This emotional collapse eventually gave rise to anger, hatred, hostility, murder, depression, despair and an endless chain of bad feelings. Like a smoldering train wreck, humanity's emotions have morphed into a mess that no medication can possibly cure.

However, that's not all. The Garden couple's ability to *choose* was also now handcuffed by sin's power. Deciding to follow God became "work." Their free will was conquered, becoming enslaved to sin's power. Working in sinister cooperation with one another, an unholy trinity of sin—free will, Satan and self—took up residence, dominating the hearts that once worshiped God alone. Adam and Eve's lives were now officially under new management.

And as if all this isn't tragic enough, their *physical bodies* now began the slow process of dying. Disease and death, formerly foreign concepts to their paradise planet, now became permanent fixtures.

Hey, isn't sin wonderful?

Look around at your world and into your own heart. This is the natural fallout from choosing to worship self over our Creator-God.

CHAPTER 2

# The Cover Up

Adam and Eve's sinful act also caused them to lose something else. They lost their sense of *identity*. Like unwanted guests, chaos and confusion invaded their world of security and order. They appeared stricken with a sort of *prehistoric amnesia*. Once sure of who they were and their purpose on earth, sin deleted their significance and distinctiveness so prominent in their pre-serpent encounter. Suddenly, they found themselves strangers in a strange land—out of place in the home God had made for them. Their garden of paradise had become a patch of thorns.

But tragically, even with the painful effects of sin sinking in, they didn't possess enough presence of mind to exclaim, *"Oh, no! What have we done? Father, help!"* Instead, they attempted to cover up the effects of their sin with a counterfeit identity and false feeling of security

"So they sewed fig leaves together and made coverings for themselves." (Genesis 3:8)

And mankind has been in the fig leaf business ever since. We've become masters at covering our sin with self-generated substitutes. Fictitious renderings of peace, comfort and hope. Like an obscure cover band poorly playing a classic tune, though they play the same chords and melody, it pales in comparison to the original.

Long before he became a world-class fashion designer, Bill Blass served his country in WWII. However, instead of picking up a rifle, Blass' mission involved something less deadly, but just as effective in the war effort. In trying to divert Adolf Hitler's attention from the location of the coming D-Day Allied Invasion of Europe, Blass and others in the 23rd Headquarters Special Troops helped design and elaborately stage an "army" of inflatable tanks, rubber airplanes and other military vehicles in such a way that they would fool German aircraft flying over England.

This strategic ruse depicted believable battlefield preparation scenarios in the weeks leading up to D-Day. As a result, Hitler was convinced the invasion would happen at the Pais de Calais. Instead, the ruse worked as the Allies landed some 200 miles away at Normandy. Nicknamed the "Ghost Army," Blass and 1,100 other soldiers used their staged, rubber props to help win the war.

When Adam and Eve took the time to sew fig leaves together in order to cover up the shame of their nakedness, they did the same thing—using man-made props to simulate reality. Only this time *they* were the ones being fooled. What they covered themselves with was a substituted sense of security, a self-induced feeling of being "okay."

We have since taken the fig leaf industry worldwide, franchising it to every continent and country, town and tribe, hillside and hamlet. By pursuing an alternative to God that offered a temporary feeling of self-importance, significance, and security, we fell for a fake. All of mankind's pursuits apart from God are merely "inflatable props" full of air, with no real substance. Consequently, we have sentenced ourselves to lifelong futility, struggling to regain that original Garden fulfillment.

> We've become masters at covering our sin with self-generated substitutes.

Solomon wrote that every pursuit and pleasure in life is ultimately meaningless apart from God.[11]

Adam would agree, and he would tell you it's nothing but a walk in the dark—a pointless, dead-end journey *until* you find your identity as a true worshiper of the only true God.

And he would know.

Like a stuntman doubling for a Hollywood star, the forbidden fruit eating couple could only pretend to be what they once were. And are we any different? Though our "fig leaves" today are more sophisticated than our first parents', we regularly wear them nonetheless. Our fig leaves are more fashionable, politically correct, and morally acceptable. And they have nothing to do with clothing. We conceal our insecurities and emotional nakedness with more acceptable coverings—things like self-righteousness, religiosity, success and financial independence. We create our own "stunt double" identities through our preoccupation with academics, appearance, social presence, athletics, possessions, partying, and surrounding ourselves with the right friends—people who boost our image and social standing. We chase after popularity, attaining position or obsessing over our career. Sometimes we even exalt *family* to an inappropriate god-like status. Of course, none of these are inherently sinful, but they become so when we consciously or subconsciously trust in them to bring us the satisfaction that only comes from identifying as a God-worshiper. They become substitutes primarily because we think they provide us a close enough copy of the real thing. And much of the time, we don't even know we're doing it.

## System Failure

Of course, some of us are better than others at this Garden game. "Self-minted" soul currency can look pretty close to the real thing while the currency of others looks more like monopoly money. But this only reveals what's fundamentally wrong with us. We have a fatal flaw, a virus released long ago into our spiritual hard drive. Our original design was faultless. Unblemished. Immaculate. Untarnished. But as a result of *diverted worship*, we now fail to "boot up" properly. Sure, we function, but just not in the *best* way. Without God, we have the ability to manufacture character, but it's counterfeit, cheap, and easily dismantled. We can produce love, but it's conditional. Happiness, but it's temporary. Peace, but it's circumstantial. We've developed a thin, see-through layer of security. And though Scripture clearly teaches that none of us are born seeking God as we were designed to do, we are nevertheless born "seekers." It's an undeniable compulsion within us. An irresistible inclination so powerful that we might conclude it is somehow undetectably encoded in our DNA.

There's a big debate in culture today concerning whether or not people are "born gay." Some have even begun using the term "gaybies," referring to supposedly "infant homosexuals." Obviously, this is a ridiculous and disgusting perversion of gender as God created it. And no one will ever offer even the slightest bit of scientific evidence for such a proposition. But though no one is born gay, all of us, according to the Scriptures, are born sinners—dead in sin, unable and unwilling to seek God.[12] This is the biblical doctrine of *depravity*, and it is undeniable.

However, even though we don't by default seek God, we nevertheless still crave the things He provides—fulfillment, significance, and wholeness. Because we are wired for worship, we spend our days seeking to experience that which only the Creator can give. Worshiping God supplies the human soul with everything it needs and wants—happiness, peace, love, security, joy, meaning, purpose, etc.

But because we naturally and willingly reject God from birth, we desperately search for truth, identity, and significance in other ideas, people, and experiences. In this search, we discover trace amounts of love and security in human romance, but it is only a faint echo of the love Jesus offers. We find physical fulfillment in sexual gratification, but it keeps us only temporarily satisfied. We imagine having peace and serenity, but it is revealed to be "fool's gold"—just a veneer, a thin layer covering up a worthless, and ultimately meaningless, life experiences.

At its core, worship is seeking, honoring, exalting, serving, and living for something or someone. And most are content to fulfill that worship longing with simulated substitutes. It reminds me of that scene in the first *The Matrix* movie, when the character Cypher (who turns out to be the traitor), is having a lavish steak dinner with Agent Smith.

Smith: Do we have a deal, Mr. Reagan?

Cypher: You know, I know this steak doesn't exist. I know that when I put it in my mouth, the Matrix is telling my brain that it's juicy and delicious. After nine years, you know what I realize? (Takes a bite of steak) Ignorance is bliss.

The truth is we are all predisposed to worship. And when we exalt, adore, and serve the true God, our *being* "fires on all the pistons," enjoying the ultimate level of the human experience.

For this reason, worship is like an insatiable hunger—an often undetectable heartbeat driving most everything we do and pursue. It's why Augustine wrote, "You have formed us for Yourself, and our hearts are restless till they find rest in You."[13]

This is why we find ourselves always drawn towards the person, thing or experience that seems to give us what we need. Like the gravitational pull of a planet, that inner compulsion to worship compels us towards something greater than ourselves. It's such an influential magnetism that even a temporary, false substitute still gives us a bit of that "Garden thrill" we all desperately seek.

We're born color-blind, while at the same time, possessing a nagging desire to see color. We were made for color, but we live in a gray, dull world. However, because we are blinded by sin, we claim that brown is blue and red is green. As a result, we don't seek the Person of god, but rather His *provisions*. But though He is not naturally sought by man, it doesn't mean He *cannot* be (Deuteronomy 4:29; Isaiah 55:6–7; Jeremiah 29:13; Acts 17:26–27; John 6:37).

Before trusting Christ for salvation, the restraining power of sin forbade us to pursue God. And that's why most people spend the better part of their lives striving and scraping for whatever they can get to fill the emptiness. We do long to worship, but we just don't want it to be God whom we adore.

Worship then is our inner compass. Our "true north." So then how does a person change direction from spiritually snacking on substitutes to being satiated by worshiping God Himself?

## Who's Seeking Whom?

We've seen that, ultimately, we all end up worshiping something. We have to, for we cannot "not" worship. It's just not possible since there is no neutral ground for the human soul. We are compelled from within to focus on *something*. Resisting worship is like holding your breath. Hold it for a while and you pass out. Do it long enough and you *check out*. Those who make the conscious choice to cease worshiping become clinically and chronically depressed, eventually losing their purpose for *being*. Then they die—sometimes physically and always inwardly.

Positively put, to live is to worship, to seek something greater, bigger and better than you—something that gives you what you need. This is one explanation for why the world has so many religions. They are all man's futile attempt to fill the longing to worship. Every continent and nation, every race and creed, every community and neighborhood are all populated by such seekers and searchers. We're all thirsty, naturally born worshipers hopelessly lost in a sea of substitutes.

Fortunately for Adam and Eve, God wasn't content to let them live off cheap "Brand X" substitutes that self, Satan, and the world had to offer. Though they chose to worship something other than their Creator, God still chose to pursue them.

Wait. Stop. Time out. Go back and read that last sentence again. Slowly this time.

That one reality may be the deepest, most significant truth you ever consider this side of eternity. Quite possibly the most profound thought your brain entertains while you have breath in your lungs. Try to imagine for a moment: In spite of your sin and regular disobedience, God still chooses to pursue a relationship with you. Allow that truth to settle into your brain. Let's travel past the front gate of your mind, past the sentry standing guard who typically says, *"Yeah, yeah. I already knew that."* Permit this truth access to a deeper, more real and authentic part of you. Hear it knocking on the door of that place in you where intimacy dwells. Now open the door and invite it in. Now gaze into that truth like you would a favorite photograph. It's one of those things that, when properly contemplated, causes you to shake your head in near disbelief.

> Resisting worship is like holding your breath. Hold it for a while and you pass out. Do it long enough and you check out.

"God loves me in spite of my sin. He pursues me. He still *wants* me."

It's a truth that can be hard to swallow. Difficult to wrap our finite minds around because, well, it's infinitely incomprehensible. And the reason is because those who have a deep awareness of the magnitude of their sin find it surprisingly refreshing that God, this holy and righteous, would consider reconciliation with His rebellious creation.

Such persons recognize that, *because* He is God, He is under no moral obligation to seek a solution to man's sin problem. Some may acknowledge God's holiness, yet within the same breath invoke His attribute of love as an apparent "character *counter balance*" as if His love somehow offsets His anger. Like his mercy exists to "manage" His wrath towards sinners.

But none of God's attributes have any need to "offset" one another in some sort of divine balancing act. His love and wrath are not, nor ever will be, mutually exclusive. His righteous anger is not the "bad guy," with His gracious love being the "hero." There is no tension or divine schizophrenia with the Almighty. Instead, all His eternal characteristics are perfectly self-governed in glorious harmony because He is God.

> "God loves me in spite of my sin. He pursues me. He still wants me."

In other words, there is only one of Him, and He is unique, incomparable, and unlike any other created thing or so-called "god." In His own words to Isaiah, the prophet records:

> "To whom then will you liken Me
> That I would be *his* equal?" says the Holy One.
> Lift up your eyes on high
> And see who has created these *stars*,
> The One who leads forth their host by number,
> He calls them all by name;
> Because of the greatness of His might and the strength of *His* power,
> Not one *of them* is missing. (Isaiah 40:25–26)

And in what is the longest direct discourse by God in the entire Bible, He declares to Job:

> "Where were you when I laid the foundation of the earth?
> Tell *Me*, if you have understanding,
> Who set its measurements? Since you know.
> Or who stretched the line on it?
> On what were its bases sunk?
> Or who laid its cornerstone,
> When the morning stars sang together
> And all the sons of God shouted for joy? (Job 38:4–7)

Later, in the same speech, He continues:

> Who then is he that can stand before Me?
> Who has given to Me that I should repay him?
> Whatever is under the whole heaven is Mine. (Job 41:10–11)[14]

Job's reasonable conclusion was that he was so unqualified to bring an argument and accusation of injustice against God that he places his hand over his mouth as if to say, "I'm just going to shut up for a while." (Job 42:4)

Like Nebuchadnezzar and Paul, Job realized God is the sovereign King over all and Who does exactly as He pleases (Psalm 115:3; 135:6; Daniel 4:35; Romans 9:14–24; Ephesians 1:11). And no mortal man—finite, dead in sin, and made from dust—has any right or reason to bring an accusation against Him.

In light of such truth—God's sovereignty and supremacy over everything, in view of our sin, and the fact we deserve eternal wrath—the idea that He still loves us is a concept more refreshing, redeeming and relieving than any thought the human mind could ever entertain.

During a lecture tour in 1962, famed theologian Karl Barth spoke at the University of Chicago. Following the lecture, Dr. Barth took questions from the audience. One participant stood and asked the aged theologian if he could summarize his life's work and theology in a single sentence. Barth replied, "Yes, I can. In the words of a song I learned at my mother's knee: 'Jesus loves me, this I know. For the Bible tells me so.'"

You see, there truly is a reason why we say "Amazing Grace."

That's the kind of god our Father is. Sovereign. Supreme. Holy. Righteous. Wrathful. Loving. Compassionate. Full of Grace.

Do you believe this?

If so, then why do you settle for less when there is so much more available to us?

Okay, that's a little too convicting.

Fortunately, Adam and Eve experienced God's grace and mercy, even after their sinful choice:

> Then the man and his wife heard the sound of the LORD God as he was walking in the garden in the cool of the day, and they hid from the LORD God among the trees of the garden. But the LORD God called to the man, "Where are you?" He answered, "I heard you in the garden, and I was afraid because I was naked; so I hid." And He said, "Who told you that you were naked? Have you eaten from the tree that I commanded you not to eat from?" (Genesis 3:8–9)

Okay, wait a minute. Let's make an obvious observation here. God didn't really need to know where they were because, after all, He's God and He knows everything, right? He wasn't playing hide-and-go-seek in the Garden with His children. He knew precisely where they were. He *did*, however, want them to know where *He* was. God's call to them was not a condemning one, but rather one motivated by compassion. It was not the call of a cold Creator, but of a caring Father. That's because Adam and Eve were more than just a part of His creation. More than just subjects of the King, they were His children. And He loved them. In calling out to them, God was giving them an opportunity to come back to Him. No, He didn't need to find them. He simply wanted them to be found…*by* Him. Needless to say, God could have merely written them off, cast them aside and started the human race all over again with a brand new couple. Pressing the "reset button," He could have scratched the original plan and simply given humanity another try. Or He could have just as easily exercised His righteousness and sent them both straight to hell. And in doing so, He would have been perfectly just. They had clearly violated His holy command, knowingly and willingly breaking His standard. Their actions were deliberate. They deserved judgment and they knew it. And that's why they feared the presence of the Lord. They expected a waiting Judge if they came out of hiding.

What they got was a Father.

Instead of judgment, God was calling our first parents to a place of confession, repentance and restoration.[15]

*Confession* so they would agree with Him concerning their sin. He also wanted them to *repent*—to change their minds—doing an "about-face" in their attitude towards Him. But they also needed to change their minds about His plan as well, agreeing that His way really was best for them. They needed again to believe He was a good God, and that in

Him, they would find all they needed for life and fulfillment. They needed to agree that life was not found in the deceptive "bargains" offered by the devil. The Creator wanted them to realize that, unlike the devil, there was no hidden "fine print" in His promises to them. In short, they just needed to trust their Father again.

And why would God want them back after what they had done? So He might love, redeem, and *restore* them. They were precious to Him, and He was plainly demonstrating that here.

> Instead of judgment, God was calling our first parents to a place of confession, repentance and restoration.

He wanted to repair the tear in their relationship, using His own love to sew up the rip in the fabric. Their sin had effectively torn the relationship. But God had plans to bring them back home to Him. He wanted Adam and Eve to rediscover their true identity. To once again become true worshipers. And the rest of Scripture is the story of how God did just that for them…and for *us*.

## Fatal Fallout

There were, of course, devastating consequences to Adam and Eve's sin. There always are. Sometimes they're immediately felt or seen. At other times they are delayed. But they inevitably come. And there is always *loss*. Loss of time, opportunity, relationship, blessing, growth, joy, peace…and the list goes on and on. When sin wins, we lose—big time. And that's exactly what humanity's first family experienced. God's love would eventually redeem them, but because He is righteous, He could not ignore their transgression. Moses recounts the story for us:

> Adam said, "I heard the sound of You in the garden, and I was afraid because I was naked; so I hid myself." And He said, "Who told you that you were naked? Have you eaten from the tree of which I commanded you not to eat?" The man said, "The woman whom You gave to be with me, she gave me from the tree, and I ate." Then the Lord God said to the woman, "What is this you have done?" And the woman said, "The serpent deceived me, and I ate." (Genesis 3:10–13)

Adam's first clue God was coming for him was the "sound" of Him walking in the Garden (vv. 8,10). He also heard the sound of God's voice. These sounds signified the presence of God to the man, and he was afraid. God was in the Garden, and because Adam knew what he had done, he was overcome with shame.

Some Bible scholars believe Moses' word choice here indicates a literal, physical presence of God. But how can this be since God is spirit (John 4:24). One possibility is this was an example of what theologians call a "Theophany," or "Christophany." Many times in the Old Testament, God appears in human form to certain persons. A Theophany occurs when the Second Member of the Godhead takes on an incarnational role. He is often referred to as "The Angel of the Lord," and speaks in the first person, speaking God Himself (Genesis 16:10). Another evidence of the Divine Presence is that this "Angel" is treated as God (Genesis 16:13, 18:1–2).[16]

> A Theophany occurs when the Second Member of the Godhead takes on an incarnational role.

This is likely what we see here in Genesis 3:8, as the Second Member of the Trinity takes on human form, just as He would many other times in the years to come. Of course, the ultimate expression of incarnation occurred when He entered the world through a virgin. He "became flesh and dwelled among us" (John 1:14).

So the Lord confronts the man about eating the forbidden fruit. Adam immediately diverts the spotlight off himself, laying the blame at his wife's feet. He even insinuates somehow God may share the blame. "The wife *You* gave to be with me." As God turns His attention to the woman, she blames the devil for it all. Although we often fail at owning up to our sin, there comes a time, like it or not, when we must. Every person has to face his Creator individually, standing alone before the Judge of all the Earth, who always does what is right and just.[17]

God then begins His judgment in reverse order, starting with the serpent. In doing so, He sentences him to become the most cursed land animal on the planet (Genesis 3:14). He also alters his anatomy, so he no longer possesses the ability to walk. As a species, he will slither on the ground. This has double significance attached to it since the devil had already been brought low by being cast down from Heaven to the earth.

Now the creature he inhabited would be humbled even lower, crawling on the dust of the earth itself. Later, during the Tribulation, Satan will once again attempt another overthrow of Heaven. And again, he will be violently thrown down to the earth just prior to his final demise.[18]

A second aspect to the curse God pronounced on him will be a constant conflict between the devil and humankind. And though Satan would succeed at "bruising the *heel*" of a certain descendant of the woman, that offspring (Christ) will do much greater damage to the serpent, bruising (crushing) his *head*. This is the Scripture's first mention of Jesus's victory over Satan at the cross.

Turning His attention to the woman, part of her curse involved multiplied pain in childbirth. It is implied that pain was originally part of the childbearing process, even if sin wasn't in the picture. Eve would become the first human to begin fulfilling God's command to "be fruitful, and multiply, and fill the earth." But in doing so, the pain associated with giving birth would be a reminder to every woman throughout history concerning the reality and effects of sin and, more importantly, why they need the Savior.

However, there was to be a second, more *regular* reminder to women concerning why they now had a sinful nature. God declares that Eve's "desire" would now be for her husband. At first glance, we might conclude He was referring to sexual desire, especially in light of the prior mention of childbirth. Yet a closer examination reveals a different story. The Hebrew word *teshuqah* God chose here for "desire" is used 3 times in the Bible, twice in Genesis 3 and 4. And in this context, it signifies "controlling or mastering," not sexually desiring someone. Three reasons support this interpretation:

1. The grammatical context. The exact word is used in the next chapter (Genesis 4:7) when God tells Cain sin was "crouching at the door, and its *desire* is for you, but you must master it." Seventeenth century theologian John Owen wrote, "Be killing sin or it will be killing you." Master sin or it will master you. It's that simple.

2. The immediate context. The very next phrase following God's pronouncement to Eve concerning her "desire" for her husband is, "And he shall *rule* over you" (Genesis 3:16). This is clear con-

trast being made by God as to whose "desire" will prevail in the relationship. In recent years, the biblical roles of headship and submission have been overhauled, twisted and distorted by postmodern theologians, wannabe theologians, and egalitarian bloggers. Through trying to "modernize" Scripture and make it more palatable to a new generation of feminists, they have swung and missed when it comes to defining these roles. But Scripture is crystal clear as to the sacrificial role a man must play in the marriage relationship. A loving, sensitive, caring leader to a wife for whom he would lay down his very life (Ephesians 5:25–30; 1 Peter 3:7). And wives should be supportive, encouraging, submissive, and respectful (Ephesians 5:22–24; 1 Peter 3:1–6). This is truly a complementary relationship. Every wise husband understands his wife is a gift from God and, in many areas, much smarter than he! Therefore, most decisions in such relationships are made mutually. What kind of woman wouldn't want to follow a man who honored her, listened to her opinions and ideas, who consulted her on decisions? Ultimately, someone is responsible for the marriage, and here in Genesis, it's the man. The portrayal of Christian men who are commanded to rule like dictators over their wives is nowhere found in Scripture.

3. As we have already seen, when Eve originally sinned, it was partially due to her husband *not* being in charge and proactively exercising his leadership in her life to protect her from harm and evil.

So as a result of her sin, Eve would suffer from a temptation to usurp her husband's role in her life. And as any married couple will testify, passive men and domineering women can produce an explosive combination. We desperately need more godly men to lovingly lead their wives. This would certainly help reduce the temptation for their wives to fill the gaps of leadership in the home. Most spiritually minded women will gladly follow a man whom she feels loves her and treats her with gentleness and honor.

Finally, God reveals the curse earned by the man. He begins by reminding Adam of His failure to lead and protect Eve "because you have listened to the voice of your wife…" To be clear, listening to his wife wasn't Adam's sin, per se. His problem was passively allowing them both to succumb to the suggestions of the serpent instead of listening to God's voice.

But because Adam's disobedience led to them eating from "the tree of the knowledge of good and evil," there would now be a perpetual fallout across the world and for eternity. The ground would be cursed, producing "thorns and thistles." Adam would also have to work the ground in exhaustive labor in order to produce an edible crop (Genesis 3:17–19). This is not to imply that prior to the fall Adam would not have had to work since God had already granted him the privilege of cultivating and keeping the Garden of Eden, eating whatever he wanted.[19] What it did mean was, like Eve, his labor would be greatly multiplied.

> We desperately need more godly men to lovingly lead their wives. This would certainly help reduce the temptation for their wives to fill the gaps of leadership in the home.

## Losing the Leaves

Adam and Eve had sinned. Their sin wrecked every part of them. Their shame and confusion motivated them to run and hide. But God found them and lovingly confronted them. He wanted to restore the relationship they had destroyed. However, there still remain some consequences to breaking God's law and standards. And so, after revealing those unrighteous ripple effects to them, the Lord begins the process of bringing them to salvation.

The first thing He did was to provide them with a new wardrobe. Having frantically covered themselves with fig leaves from the Garden, they were now supplied by God with something more complete and permanent.

"The LORD God made garments of skin for Adam and his wife, and clothed them." (Genesis 3:21)  He clothed them with animal skins. This becomes the first recorded physical death of a loving creation in the new world God had created. Though sin would bring death to all creatures, God is the One who spills the first blood. He did this for several reasons:

1. To demonstrate that sin brings death.

2. To show that forgiveness comes only through the shedding of blood (Hebrews 9:22).

3. To cover Adam and Eve's nakedness with provision from Him and not man.

4. To foreshadow the ultimate sacrifice for sin that would one day come through Jesus Christ.

Their acceptance of God's provision was a step towards faith, which would bring their salvation and secure their name in the Lamb's Book of Life.[20] And yet, they could not remain in their paradise Garden. They had chosen to eat from the Tree of Life, so they had to live forever in an unglorified state. The Tree of Life is only for those who have no sin. We see this Tree (or perhaps a Heavenly version of it) again in the New Jerusalem, regularly bearing twelve kinds of fruit that energizes and refreshes all who partake of it (Revelation 22:2).

> Worship. It's why blood runs in our veins. It's the reason our heart beats 70 times every minute. Every beat begs to worship God.

So God expels them for their own protection and also so Adam could get on with cultivating the ground (Genesis 3:24). Additionally, to prevent them and their offspring from re-entering the Garden, God stationed cherubim angels with flaming swords to guard its entrance (Genesis 3:24).[21]

## Ready to lose those leaves?

We've seen how humanity began, first as worshipers and then as wanderers. Therefore, life's ultimate goal is to recapture that original spirit of worship—to rediscover our purpose and identity. That is the design of this book—to help experience the very essence of worship itself. To become the worshiper we were meant to be.

Is this how you think of yourself, as a natural-born worshiper? Specifically, do you think you came into this world incomplete, with a critical component of your identity missing? Can you now see how that missing piece of your soul's puzzle is demonstrated by your unexplainable desire to be fulfilled, happy, significant, and a part of something bigger than you?

From the most primitive island dweller to his counterpart in the concrete jungle, and every one of us in between, we are all irresistibly drawn to serve something or someone. That's why when we are finally found by God and begin worshiping Him, we feel so *complete*.

And we are.

Worship. It's why blood runs in our veins. It's the reason our heart beats 70 times every minute. Every beat begs to worship God. It's why our eyes open each morning and why our feet move from bed to floor. Though the aim of worship for some may be a religion, a person, a passion or a pleasure, it really makes no difference. Every son and daughter of Adam is worshiping. Every student dashing to the next class. Every workmate in the office. Every player on the field. Every neighbor. Every church member. Every one of us. No one escapes the soul's gravitational pull of worship. It's part of our motherboard, forever cemented into our circuitry.

Do you long to understand just how natural worship can be? Ready for it to be as native and instinctive as breathing? Ready to lose those fig leaves and find out what life was meant to be?

CHAPTER 3

# Audience of One
## The Object/Focus of Worship

"When we see Him, we will wonder that we ever could have disobeyed Him"
– J. Oswald Chambers

I can safely say, that on the authority of all that is revealed in the word of God, that any man or woman on this earth who is bored and turned off by worship is not ready for heaven.
– A.W. Tozer

## Many Faiths, One God?

In the wake of the 9/11 national tragedy, America's national consciousness was jolted awake, resulting in a renewed focus on spirituality and religion, and Bible sales skyrocketed all across the country. Prominent radio and TV talk show hosts, not known for their religiosity, made on-air promises to pray for victims and their families who had suffered in that coordinated terrorist attack. In general, prayer itself enjoyed a surprising "comeback" to the American way of life. But sandwiched between the bookends of prayer and a rediscovered God-awareness was a renewed emphasis on "tolerance." Sprinkled like salt, the word began to be spread over virtually every broadcast conversation following the aftermath of our national nightmare. As a country, we slowly began the long process of dealing with our grief and loss. And in the midst of it all, we decided that though we deserved revenge and justice, misplaced anger was to be avoided at all costs. And rightly so. But also inherent within that concern was that traditional "Judeo-Christian" belief that America may rise up, declaring our own national brand of "jihad," or holy war. It was made clear in a consensus that United States citizens should not seek retaliation for what radical Islamic extremists had done, acting on orders from madman Osama Bin Laden. This became the White House mantra.

And for the overwhelming majority of Americans, we have responded as expected, with proper restraint and trust. We agreed to allow our government and military take care of justice overseas while we remained relatively tolerant here at home. Not long after the terrorist attack, President Bush hosted a national memorial service. Dignitaries and politicians packed the National Cathedral in Washington, D.C. It was a national time to mourn, remember, and to make our resolve strong. We pledged to remain united as a country while seeking to bring to justice the ones behind the master plot of terror and destruction. At the appointed time, the Reverend Billy Graham, aged and weak, ascended the steps to the pulpit. Once there, he was his in his "comfort zone." His almost regal snow-white hair shining with *Moses-like* glory, America's Pastor delivered a timely sermon. But his wasn't the only message delivered that day. Clearly, through the vast diversity of the religious leaders present, we were also being visibly taught and reminded that ours is a country of many faiths. Late night talk shows and news programs followed suit by featuring Jewish, Muslim and Christian clergy, all unanimously agreeing that although we take different paths to Him, we all, nevertheless, still "worship the same God."

> Sandwiched between the bookends of prayer and a rediscovered God-awareness was a renewed emphasis on "tolerance."

But do we? This belief of merging all religions into one is what theologians call "syncretism." And the practice is nothing new. As far back as the Book of Exodus, we see Israel "blending" its Jewish faith with other religions of the day. In fact, this became a huge problem for God's people long before entering the Promised Land.

## Sin at Sinai

Do you remember when Moses went up to the top of Mount Sinai to receive the Ten Commandments? He disappeared atop the Mountain forty days and nights. Meanwhile, his brother Aaron, along with roughly two million newly freed Jews, grew weary of waiting for their fearless leader to return to camp. Maybe they figured he had lost his way or perhaps perished in the fire emanating from the top of Sinai. In reality, Moses was just fine up there. He was more than a little preoccupied with intently listening to the voice of Almighty God. It is generally considered a good idea when meeting face to face with the God of the Universe that you stay on His timetable and wait until He's finished before you leave. Therefore, Moses really didn't have the luxury of leaving whenever he wanted to do so. Yahweh had a lot to tell the former son of Pharaoh. Unfortunately, though, while Moses was communing with God in humble worship, down at base camp, things were getting out of hand. *Way* out of hand.

Here's what happened.

> When the people saw that Moses was so long in coming down from the mountain, they gathered around Aaron and said, "Come, make us gods who will go before us. As for this fellow Moses who brought us up out of Egypt, we don't know what has happened to him." Aaron answered them, "Take off the gold earrings that your wives, your sons and your daughters are wearing, and bring them to me." So all the people took off their earrings and brought them to Aaron. He took what they handed him and made it into an idol cast in the shape of a calf, fashioning it with a tool. Then they said, "These are your gods, O Israel, who brought you up out of Egypt." When Aaron saw this, he built an altar in front of the calf and announced, "Tomorrow there will be a festival to the LORD." So the next day the people rose early and sacrificed burnt offerings and presented fellowship offerings. Afterward they sat down to eat and drink and got up to indulge in revelry. (Exodus 32:1–6)

> During that time, there was no "Bible," no prophets, no worship services, no temple of God and no one to spiritually lead them.

You should note that among Bible scholars, a debate persists about what Aaron's actual intentions were in this idolatrous exercise. Some argue the molded golden calf was simply nothing more than a mistaken attempt to physically represent the invisible God who had so powerfully brought them out of slavery. After all, Aaron was there with his brother Moses when God did those miracles before Pharaoh. It wasn't like he didn't know God was real. And he wasn't the one on the mountaintop who was hearing the voice of God say, *"You shall have no other gods before me."* Besides, he may have concluded the people needed reassurance their God was real and He was still with them. They wanted a God they could see and touch. They needed a "symbol" to look at. Also keep in mind the people of Israel had been living in the pagan land of Egypt for a few hundred years. They grew up there as did their fathers and grandfathers. Practically speaking, Egypt was home. For generations, their families had been a part of Egyptian culture. During that time, there was no "Bible," no prophets, no worship services, no temple of God and no one to spiritually lead them. And so many, if not most Jews, would have adopted many of the customs and practices of Egypt's pagan religions. They would later repeat this idolatry after entering the Promised Land. Once again, born worshipers replacing God with created things (see Romans 1:21–32).

And there is yet another clue that suggests the making of this golden calf was an effort to blend the true God with Egyptian religion. The Hebrew word for gods Aaron used is *Elohim* (pronounced el-o-heem'). It is the same word Moses uses in Genesis 1:1, "In the beginning, God created…" It's in the plural form, though coupled with a singular verb, indicating one God. However, the plural form led many Bible and Hebrew scholars to see it as either referring to a "plurality of majesty" or perhaps a "plurality of Persons" as in Father, Son, and Holy Spirit.

Further, after being redeemed from Egypt, the nation had enjoyed seeing the Shekinah glory of God lead them, but now it was veiled. So in their desperation to worship, they were looking for something visible and tangible to symbolize God's divine presence. Perhaps they reasoned this "golden god" would now go ahead of them like the pillar of fire had done. We must always be careful of *manufacturing* worship and worship aids as tangible enhancements or representations of God in our own culture. Candles, incense, lighting, decoration, ambience, interactive worship experiences, etc. are all valid, but they can easily be substitutes for raw, heart adoration of our God.

At first glance, we might be tempted to cut Israel some slack because of its harsh slavery experience. After all, they had little actual knowledge of this new Redeemer God. Plus, they were at least *trying* to worship God, right? Wrong. Prior to their arts and crafts "calf-making" experience, consider what God had already revealed to them through Moses:

> Then the LORD said to Moses, "Tell the Israelites this: 'You have seen for yourselves that I have spoken to you from heaven: Do not make any gods to be alongside me; *do not make for yourselves gods of silver or gods of gold.* When Moses went and told the people all the LORD's words and laws, *they responded with one voice, "Everything the LORD has said we will do."* (Exodus 20:22–23; 24:3)

Busted.

Because of an irresistible desire to worship and celebrate their redemption from Egypt, or due to impatience and boredom, God's people held a weird and wild "worship service." Included in this celebration were, among other things, gluttony and sexual orgies. This was no potluck dinner in fellowship hall. Combined with their feasting was sexual perversion and immorality, reminiscent of Noah's day.[23] It was Mardi Gras at Mount Sinai.

And God was not pleased.

But the sin that incensed the Lord above all others was that they had transferred their worship from the Person of God Almighty to a statue of a golden calf (Exodus 32:8).[24]

What happens next is unbelievable. Moses comes down from the mountain, hearing what sounds like a celebration of war triumph.

> It came about, as soon as Moses came near the camp, that he saw the calf and the dancing; and Moses' anger burned, and he threw the tablets from his hands and shattered them at the foot of the mountain. He took the calf, which they had made and burned it with fire, and ground it to powder, and scattered it over the surface of the water and made the sons of Israel drink it. (Exodus 32:19–20)

Oops.

Aaron, like Adam and Eve, made a feeble attempt to shift the blame to others, claiming it was the people's fault, not his (Exodus 32:22–25). Following this, Moses gathers the Levites together, commissioning them with the bloody task of executing those who were instrumental in this idolatry and immorality. All told, 3,000 men were slaughtered that day (Exodus 32:28). A high price to pay for false worship and a night of sin.

Admittedly, this is not a pleasant scene. Aaron and the people learned the hard way that God was serious when He commanded them to worship no other God but Him. They discovered He refuses to share His glory with another. Centuries later, the prophet Isaiah would record, *"I am the LORD; that is my name! I will not give my glory to another or my praise to idols"* (Isaiah 42:8). Translated, this means the God of the Bible not only deserves but also *demands* to be the exclusive object of our worship. He is the only God: no Allah, Buddha, Krishna, or any other so-called deity.

> God of the Bible not only deserves but also *demands* to be the exclusive object of our worship. He is the only God.

Fast-forward to Jesus' day when Rome was the most celebrated city in the world. Supposedly founded in 753 BC, by the time the New Testament was written, Rome was enriched and adorned with the spoils of the world, having a population estimated at 1,200,000—half of which were slaves, including representatives of nearly every nation. It was distinguished for its wealth and luxury as well as its decadence. An elaborate series of paved highways were constructed all over the Roman Empire, enabling travelers to make their way to the greatness of that monumental city. But while all roads may have led to Rome, not all roads lead to God. They never have. Never will. Jesus reaffirms this truth, claiming in John 14:6 to be "*the* way, truth and the life," adding, "no man comes to the Father except by Me." And those are His original words, not merely the claims of "narrow-minded" Christians.

So what was true for Israel in 1446BC is still true today. All roads and religions do not lead to God. Despite sincerity, piety, or good deeds, every one of man's religions falls short of bringing humankind to salvation. There is only one God and one path to Him, the Lord Jesus Christ.

Since this is true, ask yourself some important questions and take a moment to respond.

- Why worship this one and only God?
- What's the goal of my worship?
- What inspires worship in me?
- What factors determine my worship experience?
- How am I supposed to know *how* to worship?
- What part does biblical knowledge play in my worship?
- How much of God do I need to know in order to truly worship Him?
- How can I deepen our personal worship experience?

Let's tackle these questions together.

## It Truly is about "Who You Know"

It's important for us to understand it's God's revelation of Himself that first prompts us to worship Him. In other words, when God reveals who He is and what He has done for us, the most natural response is worship. Or put another way, we worship God because of His character and His great deeds. As earlier mentioned, your view of God will ultimately determine your worship of Him. So the more you know about God's greatness, the greater your capacity to declare His praise. Unfortunately, the image of God that exists today in many people's minds is more of a caricature than an accurate portrait. , Some Christians have a distorted picture of who God is and what He is like, much like a cartoonist's sketch. He may appear to some as a distant deity or even some kind of faceless force. Others imagine Him to be a God who is nothing more than compassionate, caring, and most of all, convenient.

Generally speaking, we prefer a God who is fair and loving, but only as *we* define those terms. The God of man's mental creation must be a God who always answers prayer and does so in *our* timing, and in the way *we* want them answered. We certainly don't want a God who is too harsh.

But on the other hand, we do want Him to execute swift justice on all who aren't like us. We want a God who passes out crowns not crosses. A God who provides eternal salvation, but who doesn't demand too much of us. Poll most people concerning what God is like, and you'll hear a lot of, "I *think* God is …" or "I *feel* God would never …"

But here's the problem: If our ideas about God come from self-generated thoughts and feelings centered around our basic human need for safety, comfort, and happiness, then we end up with a *"Picasso-like"* portrait of the true God. It becomes a "hit and miss" thing, with our thoughts and feelings mostly *missing*. Does that make sense?

Suppose you were led into a room with an 8-foot tall partition in the middle. You are then seated at a table and given a pen and paper. You are told that on the other side of the partition is a woman. You are then told to draw a portrait of the woman, the only rule being you can't see or hear her. Obviously, you will never be able to accurately draw the woman. And why not? To begin, you have never seen her. Second, you're likely not a talented artist. But that doesn't matter because you will still fail at accurately portraying her because you have no idea what she looks like. Granted, you may be able to portray a few generalities based on your prior knowledge of women (e.g., long hair, feminine facial features, etc.). But even so, your best effort would still fall far short of drawing what she really looks like.

However, if you could somehow peek around that partition and get a glance of her, or if she walked around to introduce herself, *then* you would have a better chance of representing her with pen and paper.

Now apply this to your view of God. Left to ourselves, we really have little information about Him apart from creation and conscience (Romans 1:18–21; 2:14–15; Psalm 19:1). Therefore, when we try and conjure up specific ideas of what He is like from our own imaginations, our best efforts will always fall short. Our only hope is for God to choose to step around the "partition" and reveal Himself to us. That's the only way we can ever really know what He is really like.

*He* must reveal Himself to us. And we are totally dependent on His revelation. Apart from this, we are doomed to stumble around in darkness and ignorance, worshiping a god of our fallen, self-serving imaginations. It's like putting together a jigsaw puzzle without the picture on the box and with virtually all of the pieces missing. To truly understand who God is, we desperately need Him to speak to us. When we worship what we do not know, we are no different than an ancient Egyptian bowing down to the sun or an atheist paying blind homage to the universe. Fortunately for us, God has *not* been silent or inactive. On the contrary, He has spoken loudly to us in many ways and on a multitude of levels. Generally speaking, creation reveals God to us, telling us of His power and greatness. And our inner conscience helps us know right from wrong, thereby revealing His moral nature. But if we are to know more specifics about God, we have to consult Scripture. He has spoken to us in His Word, and He has not stuttered (2 Timothy 3:16–17; Hebrews 4:12). Our understanding of God must primarily and definitively come from His written Word, not our experience. He reveals His true nature and character to us in the only Book He ever wrote.

Contained within the pages of your Bible is the real truth about the God who made the universe that atheists adore. And because He wants you to know Him, He has utilized virtually every literary device available in Scripture to help you "get it," including autobiography, biography, poetry, history, narrative and prophecy. In Scripture, you find more than enough drama, action, suspense, mystery, and satire. In the 66 books that make up your Bible, God communicates directly to you. In fact, it was written for you, so you could know, worship and experience Him. And so you could know the ultimate and final revelation of Him, His Son, Jesus Christ (John 1:14,18).

The writer of Hebrews puts it this way:

> God, after He spoke long ago to the fathers in the prophets in many portions and many ways, in these last days He has spoken to us by his Son, whom He appointed heir of all things, and through whom He made the universe." (Hebrews 1:2)

So great was God's desire for you to know and worship Him that He revealed Himself in calculated and creative ways: *outwardly* (through Creation), *inwardly* (through Conscience), and *completely* (through Christ). Then He permanently put it all in print for us to read and understand. So let's focus on some of those specifics found in God's written record and discover who God really is, putting those truths in real-life context.

CHAPTER 4

# The Great I AM
## The Grandeur of Worship

There is no debating the fact we live in dark times. Our world is uncertain and unstable. Countries are financially defaulting. Violence is increasing. Evil is flourishing. Wars are unceasing. The innocent and righteous are suffering while the guilty and criminals prosper. But lest we think these phenomena are unique to our time and culture, consider that a similar instability and uncertainty also existed in ancient Israel. The nation was suffering in captivity to a godless Assyrian nation. Judah, her southern sister, would follow in just 100 years, becoming a captive of Babylon. People were confused and afraid. But fortunately, out of this dark era, a prophet emerged with a word *from* God *about* God. If Israel ever needed a word from Heaven, it was now. And what was Isaiah's message of hope to a hurting people? Was it social reform? A motivational speech? A government grant? A comedy routine? Hardly. Isaiah, under the inspiration of the Holy Spirit, was much smarter than that. What he does in chapter 40 of the book that bears his name is simply to declare to Israel who its God really is. He tells the people God alone is worthy of their worship. But why? What's the motivation behind this worship? What specifically moves us to worship Him? And what practical difference does it make in our lives. Quoting God directly, Isaiah records three essential truths for us to consider.

### "I AM THE GREATEST"
Without question, Mohammed Ali was the best boxer of all time. Regardless of how you feel about his political views or religious affiliation, when the former Cassius Clay laced up his gloves and stepped into the ring, he made history with almost every blow. And yet, with all due re-

spect to the "Champ" whose most famous catchphrase was "I am the GREATEST!," there is Someone *much* greater than he. Granted, it sure *sounds* wonderful for God to say He is the greatest, but what does that really mean? Of course, He knew you were going to say that, so He specifically gives us four reasons why He alone is worthy of your heart's worship and allegiance.

## "I Am Great in Creation"

> Who has measured the waters in the hollow of his hand, or with the breadth of his hand marked off the heavens? Who has held the dust of the earth in a basket, or weighed the mountains on the scales and the hills in a balance? (Isaiah 40:12)

Next time you walk outside at night, lift up your eyes and take a long look into the sky. Try it for 60 seconds, gazing at the stars staring down at you from above. On a clear evening out in the countryside, with no man-made lights dimming the night sky's brightness, the human eye can distinguish approximately 4,000 luminaries. Of course, you won't be able to count all 4,000, but while you're looking up, think on this: What do you suppose lies beyond those stars you currently see? Astronomers now estimate some 10,000,000,000 stars in our galaxy…ten BILLION. But that's just the Milky Way Galaxy. They also believe some 10 *million* galaxies like ours are contained within our universe. Feeling small yet?

You may remember from science class that in outer space, distance is measured in light years. And the distance from one end of our Milky Way to the other is about 100,000 light years. Considering light travels approximately 6 trillion miles in a year's time, that's quite a road trip! Travelling at the speed of light—186,000 miles per *second*—it would take you 100,000 years to make the journey—with no stopping for bathroom breaks. And that's just one galaxy among billions! All told, you would have travelled 600,000,000,000,000,000 miles! In case you're wondering, that's six hundred *quadrillion*.

Okay, now ponder this: God made it all. He spoke it into existence, and He's greater than all of it *combined* (Genesis 1:1).

Unlike some of today's misguided self-appointed "galactic gurus," it is illogical, not to mention just plain stupid, to worship the cosmos. Imagine admiring a masterpiece painting without recognizing the one

## The Great I AM

who painted it. If the painting draws our praise, how much more so should the painter? Duh!

Not long ago, I won two complimentary tickets to a Paul McCartney concert. I had entered a contest online, never expecting I would win. But opening my email a few days before the concert, I discovered I had won the only two tickets he gave away, and they were worth $1,600 each! The former Beatle even sent out a tweet, mentioning me by name. I was honored and overwhelmed, considering what a fan I've been all these years. But imagine how disappointed I would have been if after finding our seats, onto the stage walked a man who announced the concert was about to begin. The lights dim and giant screens began projecting McCartney's image while his music played over the sound system until at last the final track was played and the man returned to thank us for coming. The lights go up and we are told to exit the arena. No McCartney. Just his music playing for three hours. Do you suspect some very angry fans might want their money back? You think anyone would have even stayed for the concert?

> Astronomers now estimate some 10,000,000,000 stars in our galaxy…ten BILLION. But that's just the Milky Way Galaxy.

You see, when you go to a concert, you do so to see the *artist*, not just to hear his music played. You can listen to the music anytime. But experiencing the musician's greatness far outweighs a recording of him. That's because the recording, as wonderful as it may be, is distinct from the artist. The music is merely a creation or expression of the musician. But it's never a substitute for the real thing.

So next time you're standing on a snow-packed Colorado mountaintop, pause and take in the spectacular view. The great God you worship formed those very mountains. Walk to the edge of the Grand Canyon and feel your heartbeat raging like a wild drum solo. It's *His* handiwork you're witnessing. Body surf the North Shore waters off Oahu and marvel at His ability to create such a paradise. Pluck a leaf from a tree. Gaze at a freshly fallen snowflake. Follow the flight of a hawk. Hear the rhythm of raindrops. Trace the path of a stream through the woods. Feel the summer sun heat up your face. *All* of this comes from Him. Creation is His invention, plainly declaring to every one of us that God *is*, and that He is powerful, creative and eternal. The sheer enormity of creation *screams* the power of God. Contemplating His work in nature and the universe puts us and our world into fresh perspective. Yes, there is a God after all, and He has not left Himself without a witness. Look at what Paul affirmed:

> Since what may be known about God is plain to them, because God has made it *plain* to them. For since the creation of the world God's invisible qualities—his eternal power and divine nature—have been *clearly* seen, being understood from what has been made, so that men are without excuse. (Romans 1:19–20)

Those who feebly attempt to refute the Creator's reality are simply suppressing the truth they instinctively know to be true (Romans 1:18, 21–22). It's an exercise in utter futility and denial in its worst form.

> God Himself made you. And He loves what He makes. Do you stand in awe of God's supremacy as Creator?

But God goes even further than just surrounding us with an outward witness of Himself. He also imbedded an inward testimony in us. Implanted within each of us is an "inner compass," a built-in database bearing witness to His existence and to a basic knowledge of right and wrong (Romans 2:14–16). And as we will discuss more in Chapter 9, it wasn't just the earth God created, but you as well (Psalm 139). He not only gave you life while in your mother's womb, but He was also intricately involved in personally creating you. You are not a result of random chance or even a case of simple parental genetics taking their natural course. God Himself made you. And He loves what He makes. Do you stand in awe of God's supremacy as Creator?

There is a second reason He is the greatest.

## "I Am Great in Wisdom"
### (Isaiah 40:13–14)

Consider the following mind-melting realities concerning God's intelligence: No one gives Him direction or tells Him what He can and cannot do.[25] God has never needed counsel or advice. No one instructs Him in wisdom. No one can or could. It is reasonable to say God possesses more understanding than all of man's combined knowledge and wisdom. No amount of data could possibly match God's. There exists no equation that can portray the limitless memory capacity unique to Yahweh. However, theologians have coined a word to describe it. They call it "omniscience." His knowledge is infinite, without boundaries or end. God's omniscience means He is "all-knowing." You name it, He knows it. And much more. Therefore, it is impossible for God to learn *anything*. He cannot be taught any new information. From eternity, God has owned knowledge itself. He has always possessed all conceivable information and understanding about facts, figures, reasons and dates. From that which is infinitesimal to the massive scale of the universe, His knowledge and wisdom has always comprehended it. From eternity, He has known every minute detail of history. At no point in time or through the ages has He ever had a "Eureka!" experience. He has never discovered something He did not previously know.

God's vast knowledge extends to the past, present and future. He even possesses all knowledge in the realm of "possibility" and theory. In other words, He knows every "what if" and contingency possible to mankind, history, world events, and even your life. Ever wondered what you would be like had you been born in another country, of another race or in another time? God knows it completely. What if you had been awarded that athletic scholarship and gone on to play pro ball? What about that life-changing event that happened to you when you were 10 years old? How would your life be different today had it not occurred? What if you had fallen in love and eventually married your "high school hometown honey" instead of the person you met while at college? What if you had been born to different parents? God sees that scenario right now. He knows it all. He has known it from eternity past. His knowledge is both perfect and perpetual. It never ends. God is also the origin and source of all wisdom and understanding (Proverbs 1:7). Even these profound thoughts about God did not originate with the prophet Isaiah, but were given as divine revelation from Heaven.

Practically speaking, as you think about your life, with so many different potential paths still ahead of you, which one will you choose? God knows the best and most excellent way for you. And combined with His love for you, He has even promised to guide you there (Psalm 32:8; James 1:4). His wise and perfect plan is for all those who love and worship Him, a plan that cannot be improved upon (Jeremiah 29:11; Romans 8:28, 12:2). Like a divine search engine, God has already instantly surveyed billions of possibilities for your life, choosing to draft the best blueprint imaginable. His plan is perfect because it is based on the greatest wisdom available. And it is wise because it is birthed out of Him who is eternal and infinite (Romans 11:33–36). You cannot add one single thing that would in any way enhance His plan for you. Were you to do so, your suggestions would only damage and detract from it. And as you delight yourself in this God, He places His desires in your heart (Psalm 37:4).

But wait, there's more God wants us to know. You may want to pause and catch your breath for a minute because we're about to journey into the deepest nature of our God.

## "I Am Great in Sovereignty"
### (Isaiah 40:15, 17, 21–25)

Read what the Lord reveals to Isaiah:

> Behold, the nations are like a drop from a bucket,
> And are regarded as a speck of dust on the scales;
> Behold, He lifts up the islands like fine dust.
> All the nations are as nothing before Him,
> They are regarded by Him as less than nothing and meaningless.
> Do you not know? Have you not heard?
> Has it not been declared to you from the beginning?
> Have you not understood from the foundations of the earth?
> It is He who sits above the circle of the earth,
> And its inhabitants are like grasshoppers,
> Who stretches out the heavens like a curtain
> And spreads them out like a tent to dwell in.
> He it is who reduces rulers to nothing,
> Who makes the judges of the earth meaningless.
> Scarcely have they been planted,
> Scarcely have they been sown,
> Scarcely has their stock taken root in the earth,
> But He merely blows on them, and they wither,
> And the storm carries them away like stubble.
> "To whom then will you liken Me

That I would be his equal?" says the Holy One

This powerful section illustrates what we refer to as God's *Sovereignty*. This attribute means He is God and God alone. Self-sufficient. Independent. Free. Self-governing. A law unto Himself. And He does *whatever* pleases Him. You may be thinking, *"Wow! That sounds a whole lot like some people I know!"* Well, while it may be true that some people *try* and function this way, only One actually does. So what would God have us know about His sovereignty? What does it really mean?

> He is God and God alone. Self-sufficient. Independent. Free. Self-governing. A law unto Himself.

First, it means God is on His throne, controlling all things. He's in charge. He is the ultimate Commander-in-Chief. Heaven is the real "Supreme Court" and God is its Chief Justice. He manages the affairs of the world in such a way that accomplishes His purposes. Look at how Job, David and Isaiah put it:

> I know that You can do all things, and that no purpose of Yours can be thwarted. (Job 42:2)

> But our God is in the heavens; He does whatever He pleases. (Psalm 115:3)

> Whatever the LORD pleases, He does, in heaven and in earth, in the seas and in all depths. (Psalm 135:6)

> Even from eternity I am He; and there is none who can deliver out of My hand; I act and who can reverse it? (Isaiah 43:13)

Now let's take this truth off the top shelf and look at it up close. One way we can understand God's sovereignty is to realize He doesn't have to consult anyone before He acts. No one tells Him what to do or controls Him. He is self-existent and self-fulfilling. In other words, He has need of nothing. He doesn't need Heaven, angels, the universe or people. However, in His sovereignty, He chose to create them all. And because God is independent and free, it means He has no inherent obligations to His creation. In other words, He owes no man anything (Romans 11:33–36). He has no debts to pay back to us, and we are entitled to absolutely nothing from Him. He is not obligated to give humankind life, breath, freedom, happiness, nor love. No man can claim, *"Hey God, You owe me!"* Rather, He is totally free to give and do as it pleases Him. In fact, He is the only being who is truly *free*. Free from obligation or requirements. Unlike our ability to choose, which is enslaved and stained by sin, His will is free. The only obligations God has to us are those He has decided to place upon Himself as recorded in His Word.

> Have you ever stopped to consider that God also has rights? In fact, He is the only One who actually does. Simply because of Who He is—the King of the Universe—He is a "Citizen of Himself."

Think of it this way: In America, we have a cherished document called "The Bill of Rights" in which our freedoms under the Constitution are outlined and protected—liberties like freedom of speech and freedom of religion. We hear a lot about individual "rights"—civil rights, the right to bear arms, the right to a fair trial, etc. As Americans, our rights involve everything from praying to protesting. People even march in the streets, demanding their "rights."

But have you ever stopped to consider that God also has rights? In fact, He is the only One who actually does. Simply because of Who He is—the King of the Universe—He is a "Citizen of Himself." As such, He possesses certain "inalienable" rights. He has the right to say or do anything His character and desire dictates. It's His prerogative as God. And yet, even among Christians, we don't talk much about God's rights. Perhaps it's because we're too busy claiming our own rights before Him. And while it's true we could never trust any mere man with this kind of limitless sovereignty, we can trust God to do whatever He wants because He always does what is good, fair and right (Psalm 111:7–8). Even when tragedy or disaster strikes.[26]

So first, God's sovereignty means He does whatever He pleases, and He is accountable only to Himself. He is the King and answers to no one. Second, His sovereignty also means He rules over all.

While on a trip to England, I drove through the English countryside with friends, admiring the natural beauty of that historic country. After a few miles, we crossed a several-hundred-year-old bridge spanning a small river. It was a beautiful, picturesque scene, almost the fairy-tale setting you would expect in rural England. Historic inns and cottages surrounded by lush, rolling green hills dotted with occasional castle ruins—all an ordinary part of the landscape. Gazing out my car window, I spotted two swans gliding gracefully across a pond, their reflections casting a mirror image in the still waters. I commented on their grace and elegance, to which my English friend responded, *"You know, the Queen owns the swans in all of England."*

Somewhat surprised, I replied, *"Oh, how interesting."*

But in my mind, I thought, *"Who does the Queen think she is? She can't do that. No one person has the right to own all the swans in a country."*

Ah, but she does. You see, she's the Queen. And for centuries, the people under the British Monarchy's rule have accepted it. However, back in the States, this notion of ruling and reigning is noticeably and intentionally absent. They are foreign concepts to us, and we resist and resent any president or government leader who operates in such manner.

But here's the deal: Heaven has no problem whatsoever with this idea. As King, God has absolute dominion and authority over all there is (Psalm 46:10). With all due respect to the Queen, by right, God owns the swans and all the other animals, as well as everything else![27] It all belongs to Him, including humanity. Including you and me. As Supreme Ruler, He has no rivals, no peers, and possesses both the power and right to exercise any and all His attributes in whatever way He pleases. He rules over heaven, earth and the universe (1 Chronicles 29:11–12; Psalm 24:1). He presides over nature (Isaiah 40:12), nations (Isaiah 40:15–17), rulers of the earth (Isaiah 40:23–24) and even the stars in the sky (Isaiah 40:25–26). God's reign is not a democracy, but rather a divine monarchy. He decrees it, and it is so.

In light of this great power, wisdom and sovereignty, can you see how the great nations of the earth, with their influence and power, are insignificantly small compared to God? This comforting truth would have been especially meaningful to the people of Israel to whom Isaiah spoke. They were suffering under the hand of Assyria, the most powerful empire on the earth at the time. Such a kingdom must have seemed bigger than life itself to the tiny Jewish nation, for it affected their daily lives. But compared to God, even the world's mightiest country or coalition of nations is no more significant than the *"drop"* of water that condenses on the outside of a bucket (Isaiah 40:15). God says any nation threatening Israel's welfare is as irrelevant as the *"fine dust"* that is left over on a pair of market scales (Isaiah 40:15). Like a speck of dust easily blown away with a whisper, so are His enemies. When compared to Him, it's almost like they don't even exist (Isaiah 40:17). Such nations are *"meaningless"* (Isaiah 40:17). By the way, has anybody seen "Assyria the Great" lately? And yet, the tiny nation of Israel has been rebirthed here in these last days.

Ever wonder why? I'll tell you.

God's Sovereignty.

But that's not all. Another aspect of God's greatness is that He jealousy guards it, sharing it with no one. Even so, some earthly rulers have thought *they* had better ideas on running the world than God. As we read earlier in Isaiah 40, God gets specific concerning how He disposes of powerful and arrogant rulers. Some in history have challenged God's authority—and deeply regretted the decision. Maybe you've heard of some of them. And God's response was to reduce them to nothing. Just ask...

1. Pharaoh, whose heart was hardened after refusing to comply with God's demands. He demanded to know who God thought He was, questioning the authority of the mighty Pharaoh. God answered him with ten special audio-visual aids, better known as the Ten Plagues of Egypt. In fact, God declares He sovereignly raised Pharaoh up just to show how great His power was (Romans 9:17). Does that sound "unfair" to you? Does it disturb you a little? It should. But before you start charging God with injustice, take a slow read through Romans 9:10–24.

2. Then there was King Ahab (1 Kings 16–22). God specifically told him not to go into battle against the Arameans. But he challenged God's authority and went anyway. Disguising himself as an ordinary soldier, a stray arrow just "happened" to pierce through an opening in his armor. Upon his death, the dogs licked up his blood, just as God's prophet predicted, proving God always has the last word.

3. Or how about King Nebuchadnezzar? In addition to having the world's most unattractive name, this King of Babylon thought it was a good idea to praise and exalt himself. What happens next seems straight out of a Stephen King thriller (Daniel 2:21; 4:30–37). God gave Nebuchadnezzar a ride he never forgot. You must read this one!

4. Finally, there was King Herod, who permitted himself to be worshiped as a god. But the Lord struck him with worms and he died (Acts 12:21–33). Did I mention God shares His greatness with *no one*?

And the same is true of the Napoleons, Hitlers, Lenins, Stalins, Husseins and Bin Ladens. Every president, prime minister and leader who refuses to bow before God will not stand before Him. Though mere flesh-and-blood men, they all thought they outranked the God of Heaven. Big mistake! They opposed His divine authority and right to rule and control the affairs of men. But, ultimately, God proves *He* is the greatest. At times, He even changes the hearts of world rulers to do what He wants them to do (Proverbs 21:1). Man proposes, but God disposes. The High King of Heaven shares His glory with no one. And because He reigns, no nation is ever a threat to Him. In fact, Jesus Christ will one day destroy and judge the pagan nations of this world, committing them into a Lake of Fire for eternity.[28]

> Man proposes, but God disposes. The High King of Heaven shares His glory with no one. And because He reigns, no nation is ever a threat to Him.

Again, God's sovereignty means He not only does what He pleases, but also He rules supremely over all. And third, God's sovereignty means He is in control (Daniel 4:35; Isaiah 43:13; Job 42:2). This is what some theologians call the "Decree" of God. This truth simply means God is in absolute control of everything that occurs and everything that exists. It means He's "got this." Sovereignty means all things happen only under the purpose, plan or permission of His divine will. Think of it this way: God *causes* some things, *allows* other things, but is in *control* of all things.

The Bible teaches us that God is working behind the scenes, bringing history along to conform to His perfect and beautiful plan (Ephesians 1:11). He has mapped out a blueprint for planet earth that is right on schedule and accomplishing exactly what He desires (Isaiah 55:8–11).

Now, you may be thinking, "How can God be in control of *all* things? What about sin and evil? How can He be in charge of these things?"

Scripture gives us a perspective that helps us here. Above all and because of His holy and righteous nature, you can be confident that God is never the author or instigator of sin or evil. He cannot touch sin in any way or be affected by it. But we can all agree He does allow its existence. And He does permit people to choose to sin. But why? Ultimately, God allows sin to occur for reasons known only to Him. That's a mystery, and it's okay because, again, God is sovereign. We do know that one day, perhaps soon, God will bring all sinners to judgment and make all things right. That's part of what you're saying when you pray "Your kingdom come, Your will be done on earth as it is in Heaven." But in the meantime, God does not permit sin and sinners to go beyond the boundaries He has set beforehand (Job 1:12). Though many things work against the sovereignty of God—such as sin, Satan, and self—His purposes are nonetheless fulfilled. And are you ready for this? He is so sovereign, He even uses sin and sinners to help *accomplish* His divine purposes.

> "How can God be in control of *all* things? What about sin and evil? How can He be in charge of these things?"

Paul wrote:

And we know that God causes all things to work together for good to those who love God, to those who are called according to His purpose. (Romans 8:28)

Sin, sinners, and evil are a part of "all things" that He *causes* to work together for His purposes. Think about it. He even used the greatest and most horrific, evil, and *sinful of "all things"* in human history—the brutal and bloody murder of His Son—to bring about the greatest *good* for mankind—the salvation of all who believe. Look at one of the first-ever prayers offered by New Testament believers in Jerusalem.

"For truly in this city there were gathered together against Your holy servant Jesus, whom You did anoint, both Herod and Pontius Pilate, along with the Gentiles and the peoples of Israel, *to do whatever Thy hand and Thy purpose predestined to occur.* (Acts 4:27–28)

That's how much God is in control.

Can you say, "Wow"?

## 100% Chance of Reign

So what practical difference does God's sovereignty make in my daily life? There are many benefits we can enjoy as a result of God being in control. Here are a few of the "biggies":

First benefit: He reigns in your personal life (Romans 10:9; Philippians 2:10—11). One of the implications of God being sovereign is that He has an inherent right to rule, not just the world, but also the people in it. Of course, some have a real problem with God demanding His right to rule in their lives. We often hear Jesus portrayed as "Savior," along with His love, mercy, goodness, etc. But His Lordship and Sovereignty are often downplayed or even ignored. It seems we still want our autonomy and the prerogative to rule our own lives. And is it any surprise? The thought of climbing off the throne of our hearts and submitting to someone else truly is offensive to our sin nature. Simply put: *we* want to be in charge of our own lives. We fear not being in control, thus we are often unwilling to give up the reins to anyone else, especially to Someone we can't see! This is sad because God's rule in our lives is an awesome thing. As we submit to Him, we become truly free from fear and are able to become who we were created to be. Besides, who better to run our lives than the One who created us, pursued us, died for us, rose again and promised to lead us into an abundant life? Sounds like a "no brainer," right? And yet, we still resist at times, don't we?

Second benefit: God is sovereign in our salvation (Ephesians 1:4–5, 11; 2:1–2; Romans 9:18; I Peter 1:1–2). Before becoming Christians, we were spiritually dead, unable to seek after God, clearly having no chance of salvation on our own. Because of this, God took the first step in initiating a relationship with us, so we could have the hope of Heaven. We now love Him because He first loved us (1 John 4:19). Contemplate these truths about God's sovereignty in your salvation:

- He set His heart of love on you before the foundation of the earth (Ephesians 1:4).
- He chose you before you chose Him (John 15:16, Colossians 3:12; 1 Peter 2:9).
- He loved you before you loved Him (1 John 4:19).
- He made you spiritually alive in Christ (Ephesians 2:1-5).
- He romanced you to His Son for salvation (John 6:44).
- He saved you, because of His own desire, not because of your effort (John 1:12–13).

All this He did sovereignly . . . because He chose to do it. It pleased Him to save you. And now we can more clearly understand why the psalmist wrote, *"Salvation belongs to the LORD"* (Psalm 3:8).

Third benefit: He is sovereign even in our suffering (Romans 5:3–5, 8:28). Only a sovereign God can take tragedy and turn it into triumph, right? But does God's sovereignty truly help us in our suffering? Yes! When we suffer, we can rest assured God is still in control. Nothing takes Him by surprise, not even your personal drama and problems. He is still on the throne and in charge. Heaven never pushes the panic button. Though your world may crumble, *you* don't have to because God's still on His throne. Also, when you suffer, you can be confident He will somehow turn your suffering into good for you (Romans 8:28). And lastly, when you suffer, know that God is using it to transform you into Christ-likeness (Romans 8:29; Job 23:10).

Remember Joseph? God ultimately turned his horrible personal circumstances into triumph and redemption for the entire Jewish nation![29] Who would've thought it? Only a sovereign God can take a *Calvary* and turn it into an *Easter*!

Fourth benefit: He rules even over our sin and failures (Romans 6:1–2, 6; Philippians 1:6). This is perhaps the most amazing personal aspect of this attribute. Only God can transform our moral defeats into victories, turning our stumbling blocks into stepping-stones. And though we never sin so we might receive more grace, keep this in mind: The next time you are tempted to give up because you failed the Lord—for the millionth time!—remember God's sovereignty in the lives of His fallible followers. Consider their example. Let their stories shout encouragement for you to keep pressing on, even when you stumble and fall.

Think of…

Moses the Murderer: Because of God's work in his life, Moses bounced back from being a cold-blooded murderer, starting his life over at age 80 and going on to become the greatest leader the nation of Israel ever had.

David the Adulterer: Though he lied, committed immorality, and even had a man murdered, David repented and renewed his pursuit of the Lord. He is the only person in Scripture of whom God said, *"He is a man after my own heart."* God sovereignly overcame his sin.

Peter the Coward: He denied the Lord three times publicly, a sinful act that would devastate most Christians for life. But not Peter. Because of Jesus' resurrection, he realized the One he followed was the sovereign God. He went on to become the primary leader and spokesman for the early church, preaching his famous sermon at Pentecost where 3,000 souls were saved. Tradition tells us Peter was eventually martyred for his faith in Christ. They crucified him upside down because he didn't regard himself as worthy of dying in the same manner as his Lord. Peter was a great man because he knew failure is never final as long as God is sovereign. His sovereignty reigns, even over our sin!

> When we suffer, we can rest assured God is still in control. Nothing takes Him by surprise, not even your personal drama and problems. He is still on the throne and in charge.

Are you beginning to get the idea that God might actually be *for* you? That's good news! No, make that *great* news! Paul knew this, which is why he wrote to the Christians living in Rome:

> What, then, shall we say in response to this? If God is for us, who can be against us? He who did not spare his own Son, but gave him up for us all—how will he not also, along with him, graciously give us all things? (Romans 8:31–32)

It's an argument from the greater to the lesser, really. If God's rule is not threatened by our suffering or even our sin, then why do we legitimately fear? If He has bound Himself to be "for us," then why do we worry? If God has declared you to be holy in His sight, who can possibly say you are otherwise? Who or what could possibly remove the salvation this God has given to you? Is any power greater than His? Don't think so!

Therefore, no hardship imaginable will ever disconnect you from Him. No sin too bad. No failure too frequent. No power too strong. Right now, don't you want to shout, or at least pause to thank Him for His sovereignty? Even if an entire pagan nation comes against you, take heart, friend. God isn't cowering. He isn't running for cover. Your deliverance and Defender will come! And in the unlikely event the mountains crumble around you, don't sweat it (Psalm 46). Instead, be still and worship this God who is greater than all your circumstances.

Sovereign in our hearts. Sovereign in salvation. Sovereign in suffering. Sovereign over our sin. The implications of these truths are staggering. All praise to our sovereign God!

This is why God paused to ask Isaiah, "Who is like Me? And to whom will you compare Me?" (Isaiah 40:25–26). God shouts to the earth, *"Do you know anyone like Me?"* And silence blankets the entire universe! Not even a cricket chirping.

God wants us to know one more thing about His greatness. Isaiah dips his quill in ink to record God…

## "I Am Great in Righteousness"
(Isaiah 40:16)

Lebanon is not sufficient for altar fires, nor its animals enough for burnt offerings.

The forests of Lebanon were not only the largest in the known world, but their wood was of the finest quality—used in temples, government buildings and the interiors of wealthy homeowners. God says:

"I am so righteous and worthy that if you cut down every tree in that great forest, and kill every animal and lay all of this on an altar, setting it on fire in an attempt to satisfy My righteousness, it would still not be enough."

The righteous demands of God's holy nature cannot be satisfied or appeased with religious sacrifice, no matter how great, lavish, or sincere. That's because an infinite God requires an infinite sacrifice (Isaiah 64:6; 1 Peter 1:18–19). Nothing can adequately appease God's holy wrath. Nothing except a perfect, permanent, pristine sacrifice. And that's what Jesus gave at the cross—an eternal, sufficient, final sacrifice for mankind's sin (1 John 2:2; Hebrews 7:26, 9:12, 28, 10:10).

And again, God asks us, *"Who is like Me?"* (Isaiah 40:18–20)

Are you beginning to see how even our highest thoughts of God still fall short of Him?

To recap, God is unique. He is not like us. He is above us all and very great. He is awesome, supreme, sovereign, and righteous. So let me challenge you to shun shallow thoughts about your Savior. Contemplate deep and lofty thoughts of Him! Worship Him because He is Great! Worship Him because He proves Himself to the greatest in creation, wisdom, sovereignty and righteousness. Worship Him because He is God. He is our only audience, and the only One who really matters. Let's be a generation with a "zero tolerance" worship policy. May we not allow ourselves to worship anyone but God and to worship Him because of His great character and attributes.

Worship is really not about us, is it? It's not even about *worship*. It's about the Great I AM. About God and God alone, the One Who rightfully deserves our deepest devotion and highest praise. Don't settle for anything less in your worship experience!

CHAPTER 5

# The Grace Factor
## Motivation for Worship

> His grace has brought me safe thus far, and grace will lead me home.
> – Amazing Grace by John Newton

## "Cheap Grace"

The world is full of oxymorons and paradoxical sayings. Words in phrases that appear to contradict themselves, canceling out their combined meaning. Of the thousands of contradictory terms, following are a few of my favorites:

> Act naturally · advanced basic · alone together · casual sex · computer jock · clearly ambiguous · clearly confused · conservative liberal · deafening silence · definite maybe · diet ice cream · freezer burn · genuine imitation · government organization · healthy chocolate · hells angels · half naked · instant classic · black light · jumbo shrimp · pretty ugly · synthetic natural gas · taped live · unbiased opinion · virtual reality · working vacation.

Now here's the most outrageous of them all: Boring worship.

Two words that have no business hanging out with each other. They are polar opposites. Contradictory terms. An unequally yoked couple, "boring worship" is an oxymoron if ever there was one. When we see who God is, with His great character and essence, how can we not worship? How can we worship this kind of God and be bored? How can we see Him for who He truly is and not be moved? How can we walk away unchanged? When we begin to understand His greatness, there is an almost involuntary reaction leading us before this One who is so wonderful. We can actually know the Creator of the universe! Hello? How can that possibly be boring? And yet, it often seems that way for some of us.

In the last chapter, we discussed the greatness of God. Knowing Him essentially enhances our worship. Once again, we can't worship a God about whom we know nothing. But sometimes we fall into the deceptive and subtle trap of pursuing knowledge about God for knowledge's sake. We mistakenly assume the more "facts" we gather about Him, the more spiritual we become. But surely there is more to it than that! If simply knowing facts about God, as mind-blowing as those truths are, is what defines Christian life, then we have failed to experience authentic biblical worship. Unfortunately, that is exactly where some people's relationship with God ends—with the facts. Their relationship with Him is merely another set of rules or a system of beliefs, and their Christianity is all about being "right" instead of being in love with God.

> We can't worship a God about whom we know nothing. But sometimes we fall into the deceptive and subtle trap of pursuing knowledge about God for knowledge's sake.

Granted, it's true that God *could* have made us as mere "subjects" in His royal kingdom, and nothing more. He could have said, "Here is my Book. Just live by these rules and I wont destroy you." But thank God, His plan extends beyond that…way beyond that. God desires us to know Him not only as Creator and King, but also as Savior and Father. And that's where our second motivation for worship enters the picture.

We discussed earlier that after mankind first fell into a state of sin, God came calling after Adam and Eve with a compassionate call. His plan was to redeem them, restoring them to the place where they could once again enjoy a relationship with Him. However, to accomplish this, He would have to devise a master plan, something that would effectively remedy their sin problem and conquer their corrupt human nature. And that's exactly what He did. But to fully appreciate God's grace, it is necessary to first understand the context in which that grace is applied to us.

## I Once Was Lost

When God found us, we were in a state of sin. We had failed to live up to God's standard of perfection. This means we were spiritually dead, a congenital condition we inherited from our first parents, Adam and Eve (Psalm 51:5; Ephesians 2:2). Because of this, our sinful identity is as much a part of us as our physical DNA. It also means we are separated from the life of God, unresponsive to spiritual things, and unable to change our condition….just like a dead person. This is what Paul meant when he wrote to the Ephesian Christians:

> As for you, you were dead in your transgressions and sins, in which you used to live when you followed the ways of this world and of the ruler of the kingdom of the air, the spirit who is now at work in those who are disobedient. (Ephesians 2:1–2)

So because we are all in this sinful boat together, no one of us is any better than another (Romans 3:23). In God's sight, the hate-filled terrorist, the Wall Street Executive, the "do-gooder" and the Scripture memory champ all stand on equal ground before Him. No outward accomplishment, good or bad, can change the fact we are all spiritually dead, guilty of the wages of sin—and sentenced to be separated from God forever. And what does that practically mean?

You might want to tighten your seat belt here, as we're about to encounter some turbulent air.

Being separated from God means, for eternity, the unbeliever will never experience even one solitary good thing associated with Him. Things like love, light, freedom, relationships, rest, security, peace, comfort, hope, goodness, friendships, etc. But that's not all. Replacing those things is the holy fire of God's wrath and hatred for sin upon that person. Because He is righteous, the Creator must punish sin. And sin resides within the sinner. It is an offense to His holy nature for a single sin to go unpunished. His nature demands it. Scripture declares that every person is born a sinner—condemned to eventually suffer this terrible wrath. And we all remain under this death sentence until the time when we trust in Christ's payment for our sin.[30] Heavy stuff, huh?

The truth is our sin-debt towards God is infinitely greater than we could ever repay, apart from spending eternity alone in hell. Through a combination of being born a sinner, having an attitude of indifference towards God, and choosing to go our own way, each of us has amassed a huge sin-debt with interest and penalties. Completely unable to repay the massive balance due, we are sentenced to suffer in utter darkness and separation from God forever. *That's* what we deserve. But that's where the *good news* kicks in! The Bible says Jesus Christ became both our substitute and our savior when He hung on the cross. Suspended between Heaven and earth, God the Judge slammed down the gavel of His righteous wrath, landing squarely and forcefully on His Son. The hatred, penalty and punishment for our sin—your sin—fell on Him as the Great Substitute. He experienced all of hell for you, in your place. And the result is that you get to walk—free from sin's penalty and power. You are now free to pursue a new life. And the good news doesn't end with just paying off our sin debt! He also promises a life of abundance—filled with love, purpose, peace, and power.

But why? Why on earth would Jesus do something like that? Why, when we rightfully deserved God's punishment for sin, would He take it on Himself instead? And why would He forgive all our sin, wiping our slate clean and clearing our record of any wrongdoing? There is only one answer.

Grace.

Five letters. A simple word. But bound within it is the power to forever change a life. Christ's payment for your sin was an act of grace, pure and simple. God did this for you because He loves you. Not because you deserved it or because He felt sorry for you. No. Even when His wrath justly demanded that you be banished to a dark and tortuous forever future, the Triune God chose to secure your redemption and rescue.

You deserved hell. But you didn't get it.

Have you ever really contemplated that reality? Have you acknowledged your sinful state before this holy, wrathful God? Ever recognized that He was never under any moral obligation to send Christ or to save you?

You didn't deserve salvation. But He gave it to you anyway. All because of Grace.³¹

So knowing how deeply you were in debt when God saved you, how do you now feel about this grace? Are you a little breathless? Maybe amazed as to how it could really be true? Feel like pumping your fists in the air knowing you will never, ever experience one drop of God's anger?³²

Feel like worshiping yet?

## I Kissed Legalism Goodbye

Pondering the magnitude of God's grace for us at salvation is *meant* to be overwhelming. But how does this *truth-bomb* of grace translate into our relationship to God today? How do we respond? Unfortunately, some who react to God's rich outpouring of undeserved grace and mercy are overcome with a desire to somehow try and "pay God back" for all He has done for them. But though it appears the noble thing to do, it is nevertheless misguided and unbiblical. And here's why. As we attempt the impossible task of paying God back for His great gift of grace, we discover more how we fall short of His perfect standard. In other words, we fail. In our own strength, we simply cannot consistently live the kind of life we desire. And this leaves us frustrated and feeling guilty. It becomes so hard to maintain that we wonder if it's even worth it. So we do what comes naturally. We try harder. We "recommit ourselves." We rededicate our lives to Him time and again. We vow to live by his ways, promising to "do better *this* time." But "this time" comes and we fail, slipping right back into failure and the guilt trap. The futility grows as we spin our wheels, getting nowhere. Unfortunately today, many churches are filled with moral, well-meaning, sincere people who are trying their best to do right. They are passionate about earning God's favor and approval through their obedience. But their best is never good enough. So what now?

Fortunately, the Apostle Paul addressed this very issue in his letter to the Galatians. In revealing the relationship between law and grace, he teaches us how to properly respond to God's gift of goodness and mercy. Through his Spirit-inspired counsel, we uncover four myths about "keeping the rules."

# Myth #1
**Obeying God's Rules Can Save Me**
(Galatians 1:6–9; 3:24; 5:1–4)

If Satan would lie to us about anything, it would be about how we obtain salvation and maintain a holy standing before God. That was precisely the fairy tales he pitched to the Galatians, and they bought it. They took the "works-salvation" bait—hook, line and sinker. But Paul declared those who promoted this teaching to be "false brethren" (Galatians 2:4). These men were deceivers who had crept into the church, convincing young believers that a person was declared righteous—or justified—through faith in Christ *plus* some external deed or act. Paul was shocked the Galatian Christians had allowed these teachers into their fellowship, so he wrote them in order to combat this heresy.

> As we attempt the impossible task of paying God back for His great gift of grace, we discover more how we fall short of His perfect standard. In other words, we fail.

Specifically, these false teachers taught that keeping part of the Old Testament Law was necessary for salvation *and* to remain righteous before God. This upset Paul so much he called the Galatians "foolish"—meaning spiritually dull or having a low spiritual "IQ."[33]

"Hey," Paul says, "you guys know better than this? What's the matter with you? Don't you remember what I taught you?"

He also told them they had become "bewitched"—charmed or deceptively fascinated—by this slick teaching concerning works-righteousness. But even so, it's worth asking the question, "What precisely is the problem with believing that faith in Christ plus good works—or obedience to God's rules—is what saves a person?" Paul answers this question with 5 convincing biblical reasons:

1. God's Law—His Righteous Rules—was never intended to save. (Galatians 3:23–25)

Look at Paul's reasoning here:

> Before this faith came, we were held prisoners by the law, locked up until faith should be revealed. So the law was put in charge to lead us to Christ that we might be justified by faith. Now that faith has come, we are no longer under the supervision of the law.

Paul is saying the Law merely served as our "tutor," leading us to Christ. The purpose of God's moral law—the Ten Commandments—was to demonstrate our inability to keep it. But why would He do that? So that in our futility and hopelessness, we would realize our need for a Savior. He wanted us to see how desperate we need for Him to accomplish salvation for us (Romans 8:3–4). Obeying God's Law cannot save us! Neither can obeying His rules keep us saved.

Never could. Never will.

2. If keeping the Law saves you, then who needs Christ? (Galatians 5:1)

Henry David Thoreau wrote, "Any fool can make a rule." If you could get to Heaven on your own by keeping the rules, then you wouldn't need a Savior. Through His life, death, and resurrection, Christ set us free from having to keep the Law. So now, we don't have to become enslaved to it again. Besides, your chances of earning your way to Heaven are the same as a corpse has of running a marathon!

3. If you trust in your own good deeds, Christ will be of no benefit to you. (Galatians 5:2)

Paul's stern words remind us that salvation is found in Christ alone plus nothing. "Pick one," he says. "Choose works or Christ. One or the other, but not both. But keep in mind that when you do, the other will be worthless to you as far as salvation is concerned."

4. If you keep any of God's rules, you have to keep them all! (Galatians 5:3)

Theoretically, you would have to keep every one of the Ten Commandments perfectly, in letter and in spirit, for a lifetime, to achieve perfection before God. And even then, you would still fall short because you were born in sin. To break one of God's commandments is to break them all (James 2:10). Only one link has to be broken for the whole chain to break. This means you are not allowed one unclean thought, unkind word or unloving deed. Not one sin. So why even try to keep the rules? That is Paul's point exactly. Stop trying to keep the Law and start trusting God with your life.

5. If you try to combine law and grace, you will forfeit, or lose, grace. (Galatians 5:4)

Place one drop of deadly cyanide into a glass of tea, and the tea becomes poison. Paul's argument here is that the only way to "fall from grace" is by refusing to trust in it. And adding works to your salvation equation is a refusal to trust explicitly in God's grace. Grace is the only road to salvation. Keeping the Law is a dead end.

Now you might be thinking, "Isn't all this a bit elementary? I mean, doesn't everybody know this stuff already?" Nope. Though it's a basic teaching of our faith, churchgoers all over the world think their good deeds somehow make a small contribution towards their salvation. The final blow to this myth is seen by answering the following two questions:

- What are you really trusting to get you to heaven?
- What is your hope of attaining righteousness before God?

God's answer to you is that it must be solely, completely and exclusively in Jesus Christ, plus nothing. Grace is free, and "earned grace" isn't grace at all. That's another oxymoron. You earn *wages*, not grace. And what you've earned is spiritual death and separation from God.[34] Therefore, you never want God to give you what you've "earned" as it relates to salvation. Grace is a gift for the guilty not a reward for the righteous. And you can't earn a gift.

Here's a second popular and prevalent fabrication many people believe.

## Myth #2
### After Salvation, Obeying God's Rules Improves My Standing Before God
(Galatians 3:24–26)

This second *un*spiritual law, which Paul refers to as "things taught by demons" (1 Timothy 4:1), applies more to believers than non-believers. This subtle belief states, "If I don't do all the bad things, and if I keep myself clean from all the evil out there in the world, <u>then</u> God will accept me and be pleased with me." It's checklist Christianity that says:

> If I don't . . .
> - do drugs
> - drink
> - smoke
> - curse or swear
> - have my body pierced or tattooed
> -  associate with bad people
> - go to R-rated movies
> - cheat on my spouse
> - rebel against authority
> - cheat on my taxes
> . . . *then* I will be spiritual.

But are those really the things that make a person godly? The problem with such a list is a person can avoid all these things, be a good person and still miss salvation altogether. You can keep a list of "don'ts" and still remain unchanged by Christ's power. Rule-keeping cannot protect us from self-centeredness and self-righteousness. It is self-deception to equate self-denial with spirituality. Read what Paul wrote to the Colossians on this subject:

> If you have died with Christ to the elementary principles of the world, why, as if you were living in the world, do you submit yourself to decrees, such as, "Do not handle, do not taste, do not touch!" (which all refer to things destined to perish with use)— in accordance with the commandments and teachings of men?

These are matters which have, to be sure, the *appearance of wisdom* in self-made religion and self-abasement and severe treatment of the body, but are of *no value* against fleshly indulgence.

Therefore, if you have been raised up with Christ, keep seeking the things above, where Christ is, seated at the right hand of God. Set your mind on the things above, not on the things that are on earth. (Colossians 2:20–3:2)

We should never equate our position and standing before God with external measurements. If spirituality is nothing more than simply obeying a list of "thou shalt nots," then any self-disciplined pagan can be spiritual. But godliness is much deeper than just having outward righteousness. Just ask the Pharisees. Keep in mind that who you are in Christ was once and for all determined by what Jesus did for you at the cross—nothing more, nothing less, and nothing *else*! It was His righteousness, not yours, that purchased your salvation and won your freedom. He did for you what you couldn't have done for yourself in a million lifetimes. Now *that's* grace!

As a result of Christ's accomplishment at the cross, God views you as being holy, and that will never change (2 Corinthians 5:21). He now sees you clothed with the very righteousness of Jesus Himself. Your standing before Him is forever fixed, based on Jesus' finished work, not yours. Self-denial cannot improve your righteous position in Christ. How foolish to think we could ever improve on the salvation God Himself has already provided for us.

> You can keep a list of "don'ts" and still remain unchanged by Christ's power. Rule-keeping cannot protect us from self-centeredness and self-righteousness.

But here is where things get a little "sticky." What you can't accomplish through the "thou shalt nots" can also never be accomplished through the "thou shalts." In other words, if you do all the *good* things a Christian is "supposed" to do, you will still not improve your position before God. For example:

• Giving • Prayer • Scripture Memory • Evangelism
• Church Attendance • Teaching a Class • Studying the Bible

These are great things, but unfortunately, none of them can make you "more holy" or acceptable in God's sight. In fact, none of these deeds and disciplines means anything to God unless they are motivated by grace and a personal relationship with Jesus Christ. Blind obedience and Christian "busy-ness" is no substitute for a relationship with God.

> As a Christian, no matter what you do, you will never be any more loved or accepted by God than you were at the moment you trusted Christ for salvation.

The point is, as a Christian, no matter what you do, you will never be any more loved or accepted by God than you were at the moment you trusted Christ for salvation. Are there commandments in Scripture? Of course. Lots of them. Does God have standards of thought and conduct that He desires us to obey? Absolutely. Yes! But God's commandments must be obeyed out of a loving relationship and heart for Him, not out of a cold compulsion to "keep the rules" or to make us more accepted by Him.

Unfortunately, this is not the case for the legalist. For him, the rules are just another opportunity to feel good about himself, earn God's approval, boost his self-righteous image and exalt his pride. Have you ever fallen into this trap? Have you ever embraced this myth as truth? Let's now move on to a third faulty fairy tale.

## Myth #3
### Living by the Rules is the Best Way for Me to Mature in Christ

As humans, we've become experts at categorizing and classifying sins. Some sins are seen as vile while others almost have a *virtuous* tint to them. We are quick to rail against immorality and homosexuality, but tend to wink a pass at sins like gossip and selfie-obsession. But part of maturity is developing a clarity and sensitivity to sin, especially as it relates to our own lives. It also means not flirting with sin.

I once saw a video of a guy who put his head inside a crocodile's mouth. It did *not* turn out well for him. The same goes for anyone dumb enough to stick their hand into a den of rattlesnakes.

But while those things may terrify most Christians, we still occasionally play around with another animal equally deadly. That ferocious beast I'm referring to is *legalism*. Seemingly harmless on the surface, it waits until we unknowingly buy into it before it stealthily and slowly injects its poisonous venom into our bloodstream. Soon we begin losing our ability to think biblically, believing things that just aren't true. We start pursuing standards we believe will make us more acceptable to God instead of resting and relying on His accomplished work on our behalf. Traveling to our central nervous system, we soon lose feeling and grow numb to God's grace.

In its full-blown stage, it looks like Phariseeism, self-righteousness, or some cultish, hate-filled church group. But legalism typically stops short of those extremes, preferring instead to keep you supplied with small doses throughout your week. Like an addictive drug, the idea is to get you hooked on the buzz of self-righteousness, and then to feed the habit as needed. Like the jaws of that powerful crocodile, legalism bites and locks down on your mind and spirit, ultimately twisting it into compliance. And your only hope is a stronger force that is capable of freeing you before it's too late.

Fortunately, the good news is there is antivenin to this legalism poison. And as with a snake, this antidote is also extracted and developed from the original poison. Through looking at what legalism eventually does to us, we can see more clearly how to purify ourselves from it. Freedom from the poison of legalism comes through allowing God to radically change our belief system concerning "the rules." And to effectively do this, we need to see the effects this deadly animal has on us as Christians. Here is what legalism eventually does to us.

## Ten Deadly Effects of Being a Legalistic "Rule-Keeper"

1. It breeds pride and contempt for other people (Luke 18:10–14) Legalism deceives you into thinking you're something that you're not, creating a false sense of spirituality. It's like a spiritual narcotic, giving you a phony feeling of moral superiority and self-

righteousness. As a believer, you are never intrinsically better than others, just "better off" because of grace.

2. It distorts the true Gospel of Christ (Ephesians 2:8–9). Salvation is by grace alone. Period. Not by works or keeping the commands and demands of the Law. Paul could not have been any more clear concerning this.

3. It causes people to major on the minors. It takes peripheral, grey issues—issues the Bible does not specifically address like movies, music, fashion, kissing, dating, birth control, etc.—and assigns an absolute moral value to them. Doing this makes them more significant than they actually are. Legalism says things the Bible never says, creating issues of personal Christian freedom to be gigantic deals. Sometimes, legalists misapply the teachings of Scripture, forcing specific verses to apply to these grey areas. Jesus said about those who do such things, "Their worship is a farce, for they teach man-made ideas as coming from God."[35]

4. It creates a judgmental spirit. This is the worst form of Phariseeism (Matthew 23:13–15).

5. It short-circuits spiritual growth. It creates an improper, unbalanced fear of God, preventing you from experiencing a biblical and loving relationship with Him.

6. It catapults you back into bondage to sin again. You discover you are still living under the Law, just like before. Nothing has changed. Systemic legalism may even indicate an absence of saving faith (Galatians 5:1–2).

7. It creates frustration because rules can never restrain or tame your sin nature (Colossians 2:23; Romans 7:18ff). Being crucified with Christ and resting in God's grace is the only remedy for dealing with sin nature (Galatians 2:20; 2 Corinthians 12:9).[36]

8. It robs you from experiencing genuine Christian liberty. Legalism is the archenemy of grace and wisdom. Legalists turn general principles into specific commands. But if all you need to do is keep the rules, there is no need for wisdom, the Holy Spirit, or a

relationship with God. Legalists fear biblical liberty. They believe freed Christians will abuse their freedom, and so out of this fear, they use man-made rules—or God's rules misapplied—to keep them chained to the law.

9. It removes peace from your life. You can never be sure if you're ever really pleasing God. You can never be "good enough." There will always be some minor rule or command you have missed or disobeyed.

10. It prevents you from enjoying the abundant life Jesus promised (John 10:10). With legalism, you're way too busy stressing out if you have been good enough today to really enjoy the life God intended you to have.

We can trust the words of Jesus and Paul, who teach us:

- Legalism cannot produce holiness. (Mark 7:15, 21–22)
- Legalism cannot restrain fleshly desires. (Colossians 2:19–23)
- Legalism cannot set you free from sin. (Galatians 5:1; Acts 15:10)

So legalism is anything we do or don't do in order to earn favor from God. It is primarily concerned with rewards to be gained or penalties to be avoided. It insists on conformity to man-made religious standards or God's rules improperly applied. It's "paint-by-number" Christianity, the spoken and unspoken "dos" and "don'ts" of a particular Christian circle. The problem is made worse when this legalistic belief is forced on others through teaching or social pressure—Jesus addressed this is Mark 7:6–8. But God calls us to live in freedom from this kind of religious, unbiblical thinking. He even exhorts us to stand firm in our Christian freedom (Galatians 5:1). We are to fight against legalism like an enemy that threatens to destroy us. And why? Because God knew wherever there is grace,

> Legalism is anything we do or don't do in order to earn favor from God. It is primarily concerned with rewards to be gained or penalties to be avoided.

there would be legalists who would try and rob us of our joy and freedom in Christ. Sadly, they are far more concerned about others abusing their freedom in Christ than they are about getting caught up in sinful legalism. Legalists are afraid someone might give into the flesh through freedom. But ironically, that is exactly what legalism produces. Through pursuing a legalistic, self-righteous lifestyle, the sinful and proud flesh is fed and pampered. Legalism is as much a deed of the flesh as immorality or anger. Through legalism, the sinful nature's power grows.

But like losing 20 pounds, you don't shed the weight of legalism overnight. Patterns of believing and thinking develop over years, so we must be purposeful and diligent in cleansing our hearts and minds from them. And that means consistently immersing your mind in Scripture, allowing it to wash over you and your thoughts about God, life, and yourself.

> Through pursuing a legalistic, self-righteous lifestyle, the sinful and proud flesh is fed and pampered. Legalism is as much a deed of the flesh as immorality or anger.

Legalism causes us to consistently fall into the performance and failure trap. Living under rules means your conscience and behavior is controlled by your "active righteousness"—whatever you can manage to do that day for God. However, living under God's grace means your conscience and behavior is controlled by your "passive righteousness"—what Christ has already done for you. Legalism is motivated from outward pressure to conform, from external rules and expectations. Grace is motivated from within, from a relationship of love and righteous desires from the heart. Legalism requires that which the Scriptures do not require and forbids that which the Scriptures do not forbid. Rules without reasons lead to ritual and legalism. And rules without relationship lead to ruin.

Remember, we are called to a *Person*, not to a persuasion. Christianity is not a subject to be learned, but a life to be lived. It's not about our righteousness. It's about His. It's not about trying to get God to love and accept us. It's about responding to the love and acceptance we already have in Him! So watch out for those "snake-handlers" who traffic this poison. You must decide to enjoy the freedom and grace God has bestowed on you. "Controllers" will try and manipulate you and your behavior. Love them, but don't listen to them. The truth of the Word of God is your lamp. Let it and the Holy Spirit light your way. Do this and you won't have to worry about what is sin and what isn't.

Most Christians typically experience some form of legalism on their way to maturity. This is due to a normal "learning curve" in our spiritual development and to our natural tendency as sinners. But it's simply a matter of immaturity and spiritual infancy. We have to keep growing beyond that. Children often need to know boundaries and what the rules are because they haven't developed the ability to think and process thought for themselves. A child doesn't know when he should cross the street, so his parents are there to remind him. And those good "rules" are necessary, even though he may not yet understand "why." But as he gets older, he will be able to cross the street on his own. He realizes his parents' rule about crossing the street was to protect him. As he grows, he figures out not only *why* he shouldn't step out in front of traffic, but also can decide on his own *when* it is safe to cross. As he grows even more, his parents will give him general counsel as he leaves the house, "Be careful, son." Every Christian must grow beyond being a "child" in faith to understanding the reasons behind God's commands. And as we do this, we discover the proper motivation for obeying Him. That's what grace does for us.

# Myth #4
### Under Grace, I Can Now Sin All I Want
(Galatians 5:13)

Lest we commit another equally dangerous error, let's not swing the pendulum the other way and conclude that Scripture endorses unbridled freedom. This highlights our need to be alerted to yet another deadly doctrine. This lie says, "It doesn't really matter what I do now because I am saved. I can live any way I want to now that I'm a Christian! Since my standing before God is secure and unchanging, I can sin all I want!"

Wrong. Seriously, this is the worst form of grace abuse. God has given us liberty, but not license. We were freed **from** sin, not freed **to** sin. Look at what some New Testament writers had to say concerning this issue:

## Peter

"Don't use your freedom as a covering for evil" (1 Peter 2:16). Or, "don't hide your sin behind your salvation." You were freed to enjoy and live for Him, not to sin (2 Corinthians 5:15). You serve a new and wonderful Master now. You weren't freed from jail so you could go out and kill again. Rather, you were set free so you could serve the One who bought you and redeemed you out of slavery.

## Paul

"For you were called to freedom, brethren; only do not turn your freedom as into an opportunity for the flesh" (Galatians 5:13). Christian liberty is the freedom *from* self, not the freedom to serve or indulge it. Unlike before salvation, you are now *able* to obey God (Romans 8:6–7; Galatians 2:20).

"Don't let your liberty cause others to stumble" (1 Corinthians 8:9). Since being set free, you and I are responsible to live in a way that reflects the character of God to a lost world. As such, our attitudes and actions should bring honor to the family name. Liberty does not include the freedom to embarrass the name of Christ, or to hinder the progress of the Gospel. We have a responsibility to our brothers and sisters in Christ, and to a watching world (1 Peter 3:13–17).

## James

"Even so, faith, if it has no works, is dead (faith), being by itself" (James 2:15–20). Our new life in Christ and the resulting spiritual fruit are part of the evidence we have truly been made new. A new nature means new desires (2 Corinthians 5:17). And though we struggle and war within, our new, true self desires godliness (Romans 7:15–25; Psalm 37:4).

As a Christians, you shouldn't be asking, "How much can I sin and still consider myself a Christian?" You have been bought with a price and no longer belong to yourself (1 Corinthians 6:19–20). So now, all your good works, deeds and obedience to God's commands only enhance the experience of salvation you already have. You obey God now for spiritual growth, enjoyment, and to experience intimacy with Him, not for salvation merit.

So then what's the balance between grace and works in your life? Think of it this way: As you obey Scripture, you do so on the basis of:

1. Your unconditional acceptance by God

2. Your freedom to serve Him

3. Your desire to obey Him

4. Your need for intimacy with Him

Having said that, what have you really been trusting in to get you to Heaven? Christ or your ability to follow Him? Do you live by a list of "dos" and "don'ts"? Is that what the Bible is to you? Do you compare yourself to others in order to make yourself feel good spiritually? Are you using your freedom in Christ as an excuse to do as you please or to obey Him? Do you obey God because you're supposed to or because you love Him and are grateful to Him for what He has done for you through grace?

## "All This For You"

Can you see now why grace is such a great motivator for worship? Grace helps us realize our deep sin-debt and the daily need for His provision and the wonder of His love for us. Jesus said he who has been forgiven much, loves much (Luke 7:47). Grace puts music to the lyrics of the Gospel. Together, truth and grace are like words and melody. And melody always makes a difference. If you doubt this, try singing the words to your favorite worship song to a sitcom melody. It doesn't have the same "feel," does it? The same is true with the Gospel. The words of Scripture, apart from the melody of grace God composed, can become cold, hard, rigid and unattractive. But grace makes the difference. Grace makes the Gospel a song. It's a Gospel of Grace. And God never separates the two.

When truth is married to grace, a symphony of praise is ignited. As worshipers, we need both. That's why Peter exhorted us to "grow in the grace *and* knowledge of our Lord and Savior, Jesus Christ."[37] God meant for them to be inseparable, like two sides to the same coin. Seen this way, the ripple effects of grace never cease. The awesome character of God we discussed in the last chapter takes on deeper and more personal meaning as we realize this great God is also our gracious Father. Worship then becomes an overflow of a relationship and a heart that has been changed.

So if you are a Christian, God is pleased with you because of Christ. Stop worrying. Stop trying to prove yourself to Him. He was completely satisfied at the cross with His Son's payment. You cannot add to it one single bit. He has made you acceptable through Christ. Period. You are holy in His sight. Forever. You stand before Him complete. God is at peace with you. He is not angry with you. You are His child, not His slave.[38] You are justified, forgiven, adopted as a child of God, redeemed, freed from the Law and the power of sin, saved forever from condemnation and judgment, loved, indwelt by the Holy Spirit, accepted, holy, enjoying total access to God, experiencing Abba intimacy, raised up with Christ, possessing God's presence in you, and having a relationship. All this is part of the beautiful benefit package you received at the moment of salvation. Therefore, you must embrace your status as a child of God and your destiny as an heir with Christ (John 1:12; Romans 8:16–17). It is impossible to grow in grace while we are still wrestling with our acceptance with God.

*Contemplate this: A relationship with God—your Creator, Savior, Lord and Friend—should be the most positive, fulfilling, exciting, liberating and enjoyable relationship you could possibly have. Grace transforms that relationship from a "have to" into a passionate, pleasurable pursuit.*

*Author Jerry Bridges wrote, "To live by grace is to live solely by the merit of Jesus Christ." I agree. So let grace fuel your worship. Know that you will never outgrow your need for a fresh, daily experience of His amazing grace. Dive into it. Bathe in it. Enjoy it!*

CHAPTER 6

# Dancing on the Edge
## Extreme Worship

*Live all you can. It's a mistake not to.*
*– Henry James*

## The Outer Limits

What's the wildest thing you have ever done? The most extreme excursion? The most out-of-the-ordinary activity? Was it bungee jumping? Rock climbing? Skydiving? Ever bodysurf a ten-foot wave? Or done similarly atop a concert crowd? Maybe you've tried motocross or snowboarded the back side of a Colorado mountain? If so, chances are there are a few battle scars from your adventures or perhaps some unforgettable moments. There's always something for those who feel the need to experience "something more." Then again, maybe you're not exactly the *extreme* type. Your idea of pushing the envelope may be to ride with the top down in your Jeep or to throw a few extra jalapeños in the cheese dip. If so, live it up!

But regardless of where you find yourself on the "extreme-o-meter," allow me to introduce you to three individuals who tested the limits in a different sort of way. They took their worship of God over the edge, compared to the conventional thinking of their day. Refusing to consult the status quo and without regard for personal reputation, they bet it all on God by worshiping Him in a way some even considered to be offensive.

These three Bible personalities did things in the presence of God that few, if any, had ever done before. Breaking with tradition, they blazed a new path across the worship landscape. And while on these roads less traveled, their unusual expression of adoration brought great honor and glory to God. They marched to the beat of a different drummer, challenging—even threatening—the status quo. Sailing in uncharted waters, their curious and uncommon actions raised more than a few eyebrows. Although considered too fanatical for some, their worship inspired others to live a more intense faith. In a generation given to extremes, here is some encouragement for you to channel some of that energy into your worship experience.

## Boxers or Briefs?

Everybody knows King David. We're all familiar with his exploits regarding giants and bathing beauties. But not many people remember the time he publicly danced before the Lord *and* half of Jerusalem in his underwear. Here's what happened. In 2 Samuel 6, we see David excited because the Ark of the Covenant, a symbol of God's presence and blessing, was finally being returned to Jerusalem. As the Ark is being carefully carried back, David is so filled with awe and reverence that he allows the Ark bearers to walk just six paces before ordering them to stop. He then slaughters a bull ox and a fattened calf as a sacrifice to the Lord. This man after God's own heart can hardly contain his exuberance. Following this, a huge processional parade began making its way into the city of Jerusalem. Leading that parade is the King himself, which is not unusual considering he is Israel's leader. Nothing inherently strange about that.

But David isn't just walking a somber march. He is "dancing before the Lord with all his might" (2 Samuel 6:14). Of course, like many ancient peoples, the Hebrews had their own sacred dances, which they performed on special religious anniversaries and occasions. But David's dance wasn't a country two-step or a ballroom waltz. As much a product of his culture as we are of ours, David's Jewish dance involved leaping, shouting, singing and raising his hands high in the air. Pluck him out of his time and drop him into ours, David would likely be accused of being drunk, disrespectful, or sacrilegious. Admittedly, his dance would have appeared pretty wild. But keep in mind it was a different time, people and culture

> As much a product of his culture as we are of ours, David's Jewish dance involved leaping, shouting, singing and raising his hands high in the air.

then. So in his day, a celebration like this was considered perfectly legitimate and normal.

But in his all-out enthusiasm for God's glory, David was physically wearing himself out, leaping before the Lord. Catching the eye of the onlooking crowd, there were some who disapproved. However, it really wasn't so much his celebrative worship that drew criticism, but rather his wardrobe, or *lack* of it. Wearing nothing but a linen ephod, David had shed his kingly garments and effectively "disrobed." The ephod was a close-fitting priestly garment. To us, it would look like a sleeveless pullover "gown," about hip length. It was almost like wearing a t-shirt. Perhaps David did this to allow for more freedom of movement to dance and jump around. It's hard to do certain dances wearing a long robe, you know. Perhaps David was so caught up in worship that he momentarily lost sight of social etiquette. Maybe he wanted to worship without his royal wardrobe and be a "regular person" for a change. Maybe he was tired of being "dignified and official." We're not quite sure of his motivation.

However, as the procession made its way into the city, David's wife, Michal—the previous King's daughter—looked out her window and saw her husband dancing in the streets in his underwear. Scripture says, gazing at him, she "despised him in her heart" (2 Samuel 6:16). Raised by King Saul, Michal no doubt had a preconceived idea of how a King should act, especially in public. She was a "society woman" and David had been raised a mere shepherd boy. She had come from privilege, and he had come from the pasture.

And so, upon arriving home that night, King David found his wife waiting on him.

> But when David returned to bless his household, Michal the daughter of Saul came out to meet David and said, "How the king of Israel distinguished himself today! He uncovered himself today in the eyes of his servants' maids as one of the foolish ones shamelessly uncovers himself!" (2 Samuel 6:20)

Imagine David's shock as he is so excited to share the blessings of the day with his wife. But before he can do so, Michal blasts him as he steps through the front door. She is livid and visibly upset, her blood pressure soaring. In Michal's eyes, David had acted in a way unbefitting a king. His wardrobe was definitely not a good witness in her opinion. He had officially become a fanatic in her eyes, taking this "worship thing" way too far. To her, he was being excessive. Radical. Embarrassing. Not to mention immodest.

"How dare you dance around like that in front of those servant girls. You're disgusting!"

But the king responds to his wife in this awkward confrontation, defending his actions and informing her that his dance was meant for God, not her.

"My dance was an act of worship and, therefore, neither excessive nor immodest," David informs his queen. "And by the way," he adds, "it seems I remember God choosing *me* to be king in place of *your* father and your family. So allow me to translate for you, Michal. Because of your hatred for my worship, the future king won't be coming from your womb. Your disrespect and lack of discernment has disqualified you."

Ouch.

Scripture tells us Michal went to her grave childless.[39]

David's "delirious dance" was not recorded for us in the Bible as a tutorial on how to worship. It is however, an accurate description of how he did worship that day in Jerusalem. But though we are not commanded to imitate his style, we could learn a lot from his spirit. We could be encouraged by his fervor, enthusiasm, zeal and pure delight in the presence of God.

So, should you feel the urge to dance before the Lord in your "ephod," you might consider doing it in the privacy of your own home. But by no means should you quench the spirit of worship David demonstrated that day. Extreme as it was, it remains an authentic expression of joy in his God.

## A Party for Doctor Jesus

Another example of extreme worship occurs after one of the most notable conversions in Jesus' ministry. It involves the change of life experienced by a man named Matthew (Levi). He was a tax collector by profession. And as you might imagine, being employed by the IRS of his day, Matthew was not exactly the most liked man in town. He was the "taxman." And along with his tax-collecting cohorts, he was generally hated by most citizens. After all, they made their living by taking peoples' hard-earned money. Sort of how you feel after seeing the "bite" Uncle Sam takes from your paycheck. You can almost see the teeth marks on the paper, right?

But for those living in Matthew's day, they suffered even more from these tax-collecting crooks. Those first-century publicans not only collected the Roman tax, but also tacked on a few additional tariffs of their own. And they lined their pockets with these extra taxes.

Working for the Roman government, Matthew's job was to sit at the Toll House and collect what was due from each of Capernaum's citizens. The Jews didn't care much for the Romans, but they especially despised fellow Jews like Matthew who worked for the Roman government. These men were viewed as traitors. Turncoats. Scum. Benedict Arnolds. They not only betrayed their Jewish brethren, but effectually stole from them as well. They were classic sellouts, placing cash and career over camaraderie with blood relatives and fellow Hebrews. Tax collectors were generally considered greedy, unscrupulous, dishonest, deceitful, unprincipled, corrupt, ruthless, and obnoxious. And by all accounts, Matthew was the quintessential publican.

But all that changed the day this man met Jesus Christ. Passing by the tax office, Jesus calls this crooked tax collector to "follow Me" (Matthew 9:9). Since it is likely Matthew had seen Christ on other previous occasions, it wouldn't have been a strange thing for Jesus to speak to Him. Everyone was required to file past Matthew's tax booth, Jesus being no exception. But this day was different. Matthew heard Christ's compelling call, not addressed to a crowd of thousands, but to him alone. Specifically and personally, Jesus called him, just as He does us. Rising from his chair, he immediately resigned from his job and resolved to follow Christ. Dr. Luke tells us this publican "left everything behind" for Jesus.[40]

Not long after this, Matthew does something out of the ordinary. Having experienced a change of heart leading to new desires, he decides to throw a dinner party. But this would not be your normal, run-of-the-mill dinner gathering. This party is unusual because of who was on the guest list that evening. Of course, Jesus and His disciples were there, but you would expect that since Matthew is now one of his followers. But it's the other guests dining at his house that night that made things interesting. Sitting at the table with the Son of God are "many tax-gatherers and sinners" (Matthew 9:10). Matthew's old "frat brothers." Publican "party animals." These were the men who were well-acquainted with the "old Levi." The knew him "back when."

So plentiful were the tax-gatherers present that evening that some of the disciples may have kept their hands in their pockets to keep them from being "picked." But seriously, can you see Matthew's change of heart on display here? Instead of shunning his former friends, assuming a "holier-than-thou" attitude, he invites them into his home. Also joining the unrighteous rabble that evening were "sinners." These were people considered unworthy of participating in the Jewish faith community. When used to describe a woman, the word "sinner" described an outcast, usually due to an immoral reputation. In other words, *prostitutes*. It's not known if such women were present that evening. But because of this guest list and other such dinner gatherings, Jesus Christ was labeled a "drunkard, gluttonous, friend of sinners."[41] In fact, He was often accused of receiving sinners and eating with them. In those days, to eat with someone signified a desire to have a relationship with him. And to this charge, Jesus pleads "guilty." He was, and still is, *the* friend of sinners.

> Matthew heard Christ's compelling call, not addressed to a crowd of thousands, but to him alone. Specifically and personally, Jesus called him, just as He does us.

Aren't you glad?

In contrast to Christ, the Pharisees and religious leaders were the enemies and judges of sinners. They purposefully walked on the other side of the street to avoid them. That's because they were "better." And 2,000 years later, they still think they are. Time hasn't changed the human heart. Religious people still despise sinners, don't they? Jesus scathingly rebuked such people, proclaiming that repentant tax-gatherers and harlots would get into the kingdom before the Pharisees would.[42] That's because they recognized their sinful state and, therefore, knew how badly they needed a Savior.

That night at Matthew's house, the Pharisees saw Jesus having a good time with sinners. He actually enjoyed their company, and that made the religious elite mad. But Jesus wasn't there that night to show sinners that Christians can have a good time without getting drunk. He wasn't looking to carve another notch in His spiritual belt as He hooked them with *Gospel bait*. He and Matthew hadn't programmed an evangelistic outreach for the evening, whereupon, following dessert, Matthew would share a 3–5 minute testimony, after which Jesus would bring a message, and one of the women would close the night with a "song of invitation."

No. It was way more spiritual than that. Jesus showed up to the party that night to show these people an uncommon love. He had come to earth for folks just like them. And eventually, many would place their faith in Him because of this love. But that night, it was just dinner at Matthews—a celebration with Jesus, the disciples, tax-gatherers, and a colorful collage of sinners.

And Levi was loving every minute of it.

These were his people. And He was eager for his friends to see Jesus up close because he was convinced that in Him, they would find something they had not found in their encounters with other rabbis and religious people. That "something" was acceptance, authenticity, and access to God Almighty. And how would Matthew know this? Because that's exactly what Jesus had given him.

So, in response to the mercy and grace shown him, Matthew may have thought *What can I do to communicate how awesome Jesus is? I've got it! I'll throw a party for Him! I'll invite Him to dinner to meet my friends. Then everyone will know I am not ashamed of Him. Then they will know that what has happened to me is real. They will know I am a changed man.*

And that's exactly what He did. This event ended up being an act of worship disguised as a dinner party. Levi was telling his little world, and particularly Jesus, just how worthy he considered Him to be. However, like David, he too caused a commotion among others observing his offering of worship. Here it was the Pharisees, who were bystanders at the feast.

Too timid, insecure or cowardly to ask Jesus directly, these religious leaders instead question His disciples. "Why is your teacher eating with the tax-gatherers and sinners?" Or, if I might paraphrase,

"Why does your teacher, a Jew who claims to be a faithful follower of Abraham and the Law, fellowship with heathens and unbelievers? Doesn't he realize a man is known by the company he keeps? This must mean He sympathizes with their character and deeds. He must secretly be like them. That must be why He enjoys their company so much."

The Pharisees must have thought they had some "dirt" on Jesus. Unfortunately for them, Jesus overheard their murmurings and responded.

> But when He heard this, He said, "It is not those who are healthy who need a physician, but those who are sick. But go and learn what this means, 'I DESIRE COMPASSION, AND NOT SACRIFICE,' for I did not come to call the righteous, but sinners."[43]

The Pharisees thought of themselves as needing nothing. In their own eyes, they were complete. They had arrived. They were spiritual. Godly. Righteous. Better than you.

And it showed in their comments. Today's Pharisees communicate their superiority in more subtle ways, like with a "holier-than-thou" raised eyebrow, a voice inflection, a facial expression, or simply by silence. Like the look certain people give you when you're slipping in late for church. It's a stare that seems to say, "Tisk, Tisk. You're bad, and we're not. We were on time. YOU are late for the Lord's service as everyone can plainly see."

But the Pharisees in Jesus' day were never known for their subtlety. They simply said what they thought, and rarely did anyone challenge them. Except here, that is. In giving Jesus a piece of their mind they couldn't afford to lose, they opened themselves up to a rebuke from the Son of God. Smug and secure in their self-righteousness, they could not have anticipated that a carpenter would verbally out-duel them. Besides, they knew the Scriptures well. Unfortunately, they were about to meet their match. He not only knew the contents and context of the Bible, He wrote the entire Book!

Jesus answers their objection with a 1-2 punch that sends the Pharisees reeling back on their heels. First, He rebukes their character, letting them know they aren't as hot as they think they are.

"As the great Physician," Jesus says, "I am here for the sick. They are the ones who need me, not the well people, right? And since you're so 'healthy,' and self-righteous in your attitude, you won't be needing Me, will you? What makes God happy is for you to show compassion, not to work harder and sacrifice more, so you can feel better about yourself. I came to help those who know how sick they are, not those who think they're already righteous in themselves."[44]

The irony here, of course, is that Jesus really *was* better than the Pharisees. But His response to those sinners present that evening wasn't condemnation, but mercy and compassion. And in doing so, Jesus was saying it doesn't matter how "good," obedient or holy you are if you don't have compassion for people. Avoiding outward contact with sinners isn't a substitute for showing grace to them. But to show grace, you first have to experience it yourself. And prior to this, you must understand your own sinful condition. And therein lies the root of the problem. Of course, the disciples must have been elbowing one another in the sides, attempting in vain to contain their snickering as Jesus rebuked the Pharisees.

Second, Jesus not only criticizes the Pharisees' character, but also their knowledge of Scripture. They were supposed to be Bible experts, fully able to explain Scripture to the people. But Jesus turns the critical searchlight on them by quoting from memory Hosea 6:6. Like an x-ray, Jesus' words revealed what was really on the inside of those hypocrites. He peeled open their chests, exposing their hearts for everyone to see. The Pharisees had never really learned the meaning of this passage, which clearly teaches that a merciful attitude and gracious deeds are more pleasing to God than outward sacrifice and ceremonies. There is a hint of sarcasm in Jesus' words, essentially communicating, "My mission is to save sinners. And since you don't realize you're sinners, I guess I can't save you, now can I?"

We can be fairly confident Jesus' comments didn't sit very well with the established Jewish religious leaders. They didn't like this Nazarene's attitude. "Who does he think he is, anyway?" And they probably left in a huff, grumbling all the way home. The Pharisees went home no different than when they arrived—blind, empty, and sick in their souls. On the contrary, the tax-gatherers and sinners present that evening left the house physically full and spiritually healed. Laying his head on his pillow that night, Matthew may have replayed the evening's events in his head. He was glad Jesus turned out to be everything He promised to be. He was glad his friends got to see Jesus up close. And maybe, just maybe, before drifting off to sleep that night, a smile broke across Matthew's face. In the twilight silence of his bedroom, perhaps it occurred to him what a privilege it had been to honor his Lord in this way. He had stepped out on a limb for God, and it didn't break. But even though his act of worship was a bit unusual, Matthew knew he was just one beggar showing the other beggars where to find bread.

> Avoiding outward contact with sinners isn't a substitute for showing grace to them. But to show grace, you first have to experience it yourself. And prior to this, you must understand your own sinful condition.

## Desperately Devoted

The essence of worship involves telling God just how great He is and then living out that belief in your daily life. During His brief three-year ministry, Jesus was approached by thousands of needy people who were frantic to get close to Him if by chance His miracle power might look their way. One such person was a poor Greek woman. Born in Syrian Phoenicia, she was a Canaanite, and of course a Gentile. But despite her racial heritage, this was one woman willing to do whatever it took to get Jesus' attention.

Picture this scene in your mind. Jesus is facing enormous pressure from the crowds to heal, feed and provide for them. They also want Him to assume leadership and deliver the Jews from oppressive Roman rule. But that wasn't His mission. And so, due to the increasing demands from the masses, and needing rest and time alone with His disciples, Jesus departs to the region of Tyre and Sidon. Centuries earlier, God had sent

Elijah to this same area to rest at the home of the widow of Zeraphath, another Gentile woman.[45] It is interesting to note that of all the encounters Jesus had with thousands of people, only twice did He ever find "great faith." It is also worth noting that both cases involved Gentiles, not Jews.[46]

From this brief meeting with the Syrophoenician woman, Scripture paints for us a portrait of someone who captures the essence of worship through her uncommon faith in Christ. Here is what happened:

> Jesus left that place and went to the vicinity of Tyre. He entered a house and did not want anyone to know it; yet he could not keep his presence secret. In fact, as soon as she heard about him, a woman whose little daughter was possessed by an evil spirit came and fell at his feet. The woman was a Greek, born in Syrian Phoenicia. She begged Jesus to drive the demon out of her daughter. "First let the children eat all they want," he told her, "for it is not right to take the children's bread and toss it to their dogs." "Yes, Lord," she replied, "but even the dogs under the table eat the children's crumbs." Then he told her, "For such a reply, you may go; the demon has left your daughter." She went home and found her child lying on the bed, and the demon gone. (Mark 7:24–29)

A relatively simple and brief conversation, right? But pause and take a closer look at this woman. What do you see? What stands out? We can learn a lot about worship from her.

One of the first things we see is she was *submissive* (Mark 7:25) Because of His enormous popularity, Jesus' disciples were powerless to keep His presence in town a secret for long (Mark 7:24). This woman somehow heard the Healer had come to Tyre. No doubt stories and rumors of Christ had circulated all over the tiny villages that dotted the Galilean countryside. Apparently, good news traveled fast in those days (even without Twitter and text messaging!). Asking around, she located where

Jesus was and no doubt ran to Him. Upon her arrival, she "fell at His feet." The Greek word for "to fall" used here, *proskuneo*, portrays humble worship from this Greek woman. If what she had heard about Jesus was true, she believed He would be more than just a teacher, man of God, or even a prophet. She recognized she was in the presence of One much greater than all those. She also knew herself and her desperate need. Bowing down before Him all the way to His feet, she knew only God would be sufficient help to her in this time of great need.

And what motivated her to come to Christ in this way? Mark tells us it was a family crisis that brought about this encounter. And can you blame her? It's often during those "9-1-1 moments" when we find ourselves on a collision course with life's impossible circumstances. And in those times, we are driven to our knees and recognize our need for Divine intervention. It may be a financial crisis, sickness, terminal illness, or even the death of someone close to us. It could be a dating or marital relationship, or like this woman, a situation involving a son or daughter. But sooner or later, life has a way of wedging us squarely between the proverbial "rock and hard place." As if caught in a violent thunderstorm, there seems no way out. And what makes many of these crises so difficult is they are typically beyond our control. In times like these, we find ourselves helpless and often without hope.

We don't know how, why or for how long this little girl was demon-possessed. But we do know she wasn't mentally disturbed or emotionally depressed. Worse, this girl's heart and mind were under the control of a satanic entity. An evil spirit had taken up residence in her. Perhaps it came as a result of her family's pagan religion. Being a Canaanite, she may have been a worshiper of Astarte or some other pagan deity prevalent among her people in that region. Mark doesn't tell us. This woman may have been a single parent and this girl her only child. Scripture calls her a "little daughter." Six, eight, eleven years old? Who knows? But we do know this mother loved her baby girl very much. We parents know when it comes to our kids, no amount of money, effort, energy, embarrassment, or loss of reputation is worth more than your child's life. All that matters at the moment is that a mom or dad does whatever it takes to get help for her or his child. That is what's happening here.

Yes, she was desperate that day, rushing into Jesus' presence as soon as she heard about Him.[47] There was a spirit of immediacy, urgency and priority about her situation. She may have already exhausted every other means of help and hope for her daughter. Perhaps disillusioned with her own god's inability to intervene, she turns to this Jewish teacher as her last hope. But no matter what her previous path, her focus of worship had finally found the right object.

This woman was in relentless pursuit of Jesus. Matthew tells us she "kept shouting out after the disciples," hounding them until she got an audience with the Lord.[48] Finally making it to Him, she continued with that same persistence (Mark 7:26). She knew her only hope was Jesus, being convinced that nothing and no one else would do. Literally begging Him, she knew her predicament required a "God-sized" solution. This demon-possession was something unmistakably suited for His resources. So she kept on asking Him for help.

In reality, this Gentile woman's faith in Jesus was enormous. Her awareness of her need and her basic knowledge of who He was led her to worship and exercise great faith. Too often, we worry much and trust little, don't we? We wait until things are out of control to seek, worship and trust Him. But perhaps we should come to the end of our rope at the *beginning* of our rope. We tend to exhaust our own resources first. When things get critical, we then start trusting God. We try to fix it ourselves before finally concluding that what we have simply isn't enough. Our strength just won't cut it. It never will.

We wait far too late to get desperate.

Truthfully, we need a lot more "desperation" in our worship. We need to practice recognizing Him as the only source of all our needs.

What about you? Do you see Jesus as the only hope for your life? What about your relationships? Your family? Ministry? Future? If so, just how desperate are you in your prayer life? Do you worship him like He's all you've got? Or do you depend on your own ability, personality, resources, or natural giftedness?

This generation needs a wake up call to worship God in a way that *screams* towards Heaven, "Father, we'll trust You to do God-size things in, around, and for us!" This is the kind of faith-worship that trusts Him for things way beyond our reach.

Though this woman's knowledge of Jesus wasn't as extensive as ours, she apparently did know He was the "Son of David" (i.e. the Messiah) and that He had power to heal. She also called Him "Lord." Her attitude of worship was elementary, with a childlike purity and innocence. It wasn't yet corrupted by external religion or by man-made formulas. She didn't follow proper prayer "protocol." She knew just enough to know who He was and what He could do for her. Even so, this simple, desperate act of worship and faith ultimately affected and inspired others (Matthew 15:29–31).

It's not how theologically smart we are that impresses God. Rather, it's how much we abandon ourselves to Him that really matters. This woman bridged the gap between head knowledge about God and experiential worship of Him. Because her faith wasn't based on much information about Christ, she was forced to exercise greater trust in Him. She took what little knowledge she had, threw herself at His feet in worship, and glorified Him through simply believing. Don't misunderstand. We should grow in our knowledge of God daily. This must be a huge priority for us, because as we grow in our knowledge of God, our faith and worship intensity can grow proportionately. But you don't need a degree in theology to worship and honor Him.

> *It's not how theologically smart we are that impresses God. Rather, it's how much we abandon ourselves to Him that really matters.*

But the Syrophoenician woman's story doesn't end here. To the contrary, she was just getting started with her pursuit of Jesus. Certainly, some people thought she was taking her worship too far. And surprisingly, she faced opposition from both Jesus' disciples and the Lord Himself, as even Christ didn't acknowledge her at first. Her repeated pleas were met with total silence. Matthew tells us:

> But He did not answer her a word. And His disciples came to Him and kept asking Him, saying, "Send her away, for she is shouting out after us." But He answered and said, "I was sent only to the lost sheep of the house of Israel." (Matthew 15:23–24)

Keep in mind, this Canaanite woman already had three strikes against her.

- Strike one: She was a Gentile,
- Strike two: She was a woman, and
- Strike three: She was a descendent of a people God had told Israel to "utterly destroy" (Deuteronomy 7:2).

Three strikes and you're out, right? Apparently, no one had explained the rules of spiritual baseball to this lady. Anyone can come to Christ when there is no risk and when there are automatic results. If it were easy, then everybody would be doing it, right? The question was "How *bad* did she want Christ's power on her behalf?" So Jesus first tested her with silence (Matthew 15:23). Can you picture this scene in your mind? Here is a woman imploring Jesus to deliver her daughter from a demon, and she is met by stone silence from the Savior. Jesus appears to be completely ignoring her. He says nothing. Not a word. Doesn't this sound cold? Uncaring? Distant? Aloof? Chauvinistic? She came to the Great Physician on behalf of her daughter, and she was getting zero response from Him. Nevertheless, she continued in her desperation worship, even though it seems like Jesus really doesn't care to receive her worship. So what's the deal here?

> Silence does not signify inactivity. The quiet doesn't mean He has quit on us. Nor does it mean He is idle, sluggish or apathetic. It only means He isn't answering or responding to us according to our preferred method and timetable.

Have you ever had a similar experience like that with God? Have you ever prayed sincerely and passionately about something, and yet your prayers went unanswered? It's like God wasn't even listening. Like He didn't care. Life blindsided you with pain or tragedy, and you cried out to Him only to receive silence in return.

Where was the heart of compassion Christ had shown to others, like the tax-gatherers and sinners? Where was the "come unto Me all of you who are weary and heavy laden"?[49] Honestly, had you been her, how would you have felt? Hurt? Disappointed? Frustrated? Angry? Abandoned? Embarrassed? Confused? Would you have become bitter or resentful towards Jesus? Perhaps stormed away in angry disillusionment and disbelief. She could have acted the same way, spreading word that the Loving Savior was neither. Instead of Him being kind and willing to help others, she could have given up, telling her world He was unloving, aloof, and probably powerless to help. She could have tried to ruin His reputation. Or she could have just shut up and gone quietly back home.

But she didn't.

Because of her deep love for her daughter and her tenacious pursuit of Jesus, the Lord's silence failed to deter or silence her. Strangely enough, it only strengthened her resolve to keep asking Him for what she needed and wanted.[50] She staked her ground in submission at His feet. She had no way of knowing this is exactly the kind of extreme persistence God really values. Fortunately for her—and us!—Heaven's silence and lack of immediate response does not mean He isn't listening or working. Silence does not signify inactivity. The quiet doesn't mean He has quit on us. Nor does it mean He is idle, sluggish or apathetic. It only means He isn't answering or responding to us according to our preferred method and timetable. After thousands of years dealing with humanity, His ways are still not our ways![51] Jesus' refusal to answer would have discouraged others, shutting down their request. But not this woman. She hung in there. She knew everything would be okay if she just stayed there with Him.

The disciples, taking what they *think* is a cue from the Lord, begin hounding Him to send this nuisance away. She had nothing going in her favor except a belief in Him and a love for her daughter. The odds were stacked against her. Her racial heritage worked against her. As a woman, she suffered a great social disadvantage in a male-dominated society. And as if that wasn't enough, Satan had control of her little daughter! And hope faded as Jesus and company seemed to be opposing her.

But in spite of all this, she refused to go away. On the contrary, her determination to convince Christ only intensified. And that quality outranked all her obstacles. Her style was extreme, unorthodox, unfashionable, and even unacceptable. But what happens next almost makes Jesus' previous silence seem minor in comparison. For Jesus to simply say nothing would have been better than what He says next.

"It is not right to take the children's bread and toss it to the dogs." (Mark 7:27)

We don't even have to debate this is one of Jesus' "hard sayings." What could He possibly have meant by such a statement? And why would He say such a thing to a hurting woman like this?

It's important to unpack His words in order to better understand them. They also are a critical part of this true story. To begin, the word "dog" Jesus uses does not refer to the mongrel or scavenger animal we typically associate with that time. Instead, the word refers to a household pet or puppy. Jesus is not intentionally being rude to this woman, but rather He is testing her faith through drawing an important comparison concerning His primary calling to the Jewish people.[52]

But the testing of her faith involved Jesus seeing something in her no one else could see. With all-knowing eyes, Jesus sees a great faith in her that would not go quietly or die easily. Her unwillingness to let Jesus go teaches us that our disappointment with God forces us to worship Him by faith without any outward or visible confirmation from Heaven. There are times in our lives when there are literally no signs of hope, no visible reasons to carry on. No feelings. No sight. Nothing solid on which to stand. And that can be one of life's more terrifying experiences. In such times, your only assurance is the promise of Scripture and the presence of the Savior. His written guarantee and His witness in your heart. That's it. But here's the big question.

Is that enough for you?

If all you had in your darkest hour was the truth of God's Word and the confidence that He is still with you, could you survive on that? Devoid of all signs of hope or help in those seasons of life, would you *still* choose to worship Him? Like Job, you may think, "Though he slay me, yet will I hope in him."[53] But that's where we sometimes find ourselves, isn't it? So will you still choose to chase God, even when Heaven seems to ignore you? In the silence, how will you respond? Will you allow it to overtake you, or will you fill that silence with your worship of Him?

So, how did her faith pay off? How does the story end? What did she do?

Knowing that even a tiny portion of His great power would be more than enough for her daughter's problem, she persisted.

"Yes, Lord," she replied, "but even the dogs under the table eat the children's crumbs" (Mark 7:28).

Wow! What insight! What persistence! What faith! But such was her vision of this "Son of David." And that's exactly what extreme worship does for us. It imparts 20/20 vision. Obviously, we don't casually or callously deny the reality of our struggle. But worshiping God this way opens our eyes to seeing the greatness of God. It takes us to the intersection where real life and faith collide. It says, "My need is huge, but my God can do it!"

It is the same kind of glory Joshua and Caleb brought to God. After spying out the Promised Land (Numbers 13), ten of the twelve spies who surveyed the land only saw the size of their enemy. But Joshua and Caleb were focused instead on the size of their God.

In our personal struggles, we have a choice to make. We can focus on our terrible reality or on His tremendous resources. We can become preoccupied with the size of our struggles or on the sufficiency of our God (Matthew 15:27–28, Mark 7:28; Hebrews 17:19). Extreme worship isn't mindless emotion. It has a laser focus on Jesus Christ. Focusing your attention on Christ's sufficiency causes you to see how possible the impossible can be.

> In our personal struggles, we have a choice to make. We can focus on our terrible reality or on His tremendous resources.

But for many of us, it's not a problem of "can He" but rather "will He." And will He . . . for me? In this story, the Syrophoenecian woman took Christ's own words, interacted with them, and laid them right back down at His feet where she was worshiping. She took God at His word in spite of everything she saw, heard, and felt.

So what has God said about your particular life situation? Is there a need He has promised to meet but hasn't yet? Are you at his feet reminding Him of His promises? Or have you given up?

This woman's extreme worship and great trust touched His heart and moved His hand (Matthew 15:28; Mark 7:29–30). Check this out.

> Then he told her, "For such a reply, you may go; the demon has left your daughter." She went home and found her child lying on the bed, and the demon gone. (Mark 7:29–30)

Matthew adds, *"O woman, your faith is great; be it done for you as you wish"* (Matthew 15:28). This woman's extreme, unrelenting faith and worship struck a chord deep within the heart of Jesus. And He rewarded her by delivering her daughter from this demon. So sovereign is Jesus that He does this simply with a word!

Picture the celebration in her house that evening. Imagine how her faith must have grown even more as a result of this miracle. Imagine how her heart must have bonded to Jesus because of this faith-infused worship experience.

Can you identify with this woman's desperation? Will you pursue Him in faith until He answers your prayer and comes through for you? Will you have the kind of worship that won't stop dancing for God and isn't afraid to celebrate? Is yours the kind of worship that won't keep quiet about Jesus among your friends? Will you play it safe, or will you go for broke and be an extreme worshiper when it really counts?

Don't be afraid to take your worship "over the edge!"

CHAPTER 7

# When Little is Much
## Sacrificial Worship

> If Jesus Christ be God and died for me, then there is no sacrifice too great I can make for Him.
> – C. T. Studd

## Stayin' Alive

We live in a misguided world. A planet where morality has been redefined and common sense has vanished somewhere in a maze of political correctness. The global economic and geopolitical climate remains unstable and volatile, only one major event away from catastrophe. All across the world, people long for some reliable compass to give them direction and hope. Whether from within or from some external experience, that innate desire to bring meaning to life and be a part of something greater than yourself still motivates millions to search for "something more."

Ours is an age where barbaric, hate-filled terrorists blow themselves up for evil and misguided causes. It's an era where cowards kill hundreds through kamikaze-like missions. Deluded and depraved, they kill themselves and others in the name of a false god, only to discover at death who the real God is. These terrorists have twisted the concepts of martyrdom and sacrifice. Even so, their fanaticism, though demonically inspired, portrays a far greater dedication for their god than many Christians give for Christ.

So where then is the authentic sacrifice for the one true God? Where is the revolutionary dedication so prevalent among those first-century believers? Granted, there are times when worshiping isn't easy. But if we only worship when it is convenient, then it's just a leisure activity, and not true worship. Sometimes, God asks us to sacrifice for Him, even when we don't feel we have anything to give. And, occasionally, the sacrifices He asks for are great. They are the kind that truly cost something. These sacrifices of worship require a death to self and an attitude that no price is too high to pay for such a worthy God as He. But what might motivate such worship? And is the cost challenges that accompany such worship really worth the price we pay? Put another way, is it worth it to worship when it hurts?

> Terrorists have twisted the concepts of martyrdom and sacrifice. Even so, their fanaticism, though demonically inspired, portrays a far greater dedication for their god than many Christians give for Christ.

Of course, sacrificing for God is easy to talk about, but when the pain kicks in, it's a different story. In this chapter, we meet two very different people who, in their own unique way, displayed costly acts of worship. But what prompted such great offerings from them? What made them want to give so much of themselves to God? And what were the rewards of their worship?

## "Mitey" Sacrifice

One day, Jesus took His disciples to the Jewish Temple. While there, they sat and observed worshipers coming and going. Part of the temple contained an area known as "The Court of the Women," a large open space where worshipers came to pay temple tax and give free will offerings. It was like the tithes and offerings of today, only they didn't "pass the plate." Because it was such a public gathering place, this area afforded the self-righteous a golden opportunity to showcase their large financial contributions, which came with immediate recognition from onlookers. Having their good deeds seen by others was somewhat of a Pharisaical "aphrodisiac" (Matthew 6:1–2). Mark picks up the story for us here.

Jesus sat down opposite the place where the offerings were put and watched the crowd putting their money into the temple treasury. Many rich people threw in large amounts.

But a poor widow came and put in two very small copper coins, worth only a fraction of a penny.

Calling his disciples to him, Jesus said, "I tell you the truth, this poor widow has put more into the treasury than all the others. They all gave out of their wealth; but she, out of her poverty, put in everything—all she had to live on." (Mark 12:41–44 NIV)

During Bible times, most people fell under the category of "poor peasants." Life really didn't hold much promise for the average person. For them, employment usually meant working a menial trade—usually manual labor—for long hours each day and for minimal wages. And if you were unable to do that, you begged for what you could get. Those who were sick, lame, blind, or unwilling to work were dependent on the kindness and generosity of others. Unlike our current society in which virtually anyone can get a decent-paying job doing something, there wasn't any unemployment or welfare office in those days. If you didn't work, farm or beg, you didn't eat. And if you were a woman whose husband had died, your chief source of income was buried right along with him.

With that as background, this woman's predicament makes more sense. We are not told if she was old or young, recently widowed or if she had been without a husband for some time. We only know her husband had died, and she had not remarried. She most likely lives alone, and the description Jesus and Mark use—"poor widow"—is almost proverbial for one whose financial portfolio was anything but enviable. She was practically destitute and among the lowest of the economic classes. As such, she would be a most unlikely candidate to contribute anything at all to the temple treasury. But as Jesus and His friends observed that day, she walks over to the wall where 13 trumpet-shaped chests are hung to receive the offerings and donations. Into one, she drops two small copper coins. "Mites" were the smallest of Jewish coins, each valued at about one-fourth of a cent or about 1/64 of an average day's wage. The "mite" took its name from its extreme smallness, and is derived from the Greek *lepton*, meaning "thin." Mark adds an explanation of the word for his Roman readers, using the Greek *kodrantes* from the Latin *quadrans*, meaning "the fourth part." So her total offering was the modern day equivalent of about $1.50. Two very thin coins. A pitiful offering, right? Not much chance they'll name the new "Family Life Center" after her. In fact, her contribution was practically insignificant. After all, what can a fraction of a penny buy? How important could it be compared to the large amounts the big givers were dropping into the offering bucket? Jesus answers that question for us.

> "I tell you the truth, this poor widow has put more into the treasury then all the others." (Mark 12:43).

When you don't have very much to contribute, giving a little means a lot. When you wreck the only car you have, it's a big deal. When your only home burns to the ground, it's a huge loss. When you spend the last $30 in your checking account on groceries, that's a big deal. Some people inherit wealth from family, but for most of us, we get our money the old fashioned way—we earn it. What is a lot of money to some is just pocket change to others. But this also highlights the fact that money is a relative thing. It's all a matter of perspective, really.

For many years, my non-profit ministry was largely dependent on the financial donations from those who believed in my ministry. One evening when my boys were young, I shared with the family our need for more donors to our ministry because we were facing some challenging times. The next morning before breakfast, there was a knock at the front door. There, on the doormat, I discovered a single envelope. Opening it, I found eleven one-dollar bills inside. A note accompanied it, which read, in a 9-year-old's chicken-scratch writing,

## "Dad, I don't want it back."

My youngest son had emptied his piggy bank, giving every last dollar towards the Lord's work. During breakfast, I announced to my family that I had another prayer request. I told them I was having lunch that day with the most important donor to our ministry. Around 11:20 a.m., I showed up at my son's school, checked him out, and took him to get pizza.

"But, dad," he inquired, "I though you said you were having lunch with your most important donor today."

I replied, "Yep. And that's exactly what I am doing, son."

His face could hardly contain the huge grin that stretched from ear to ear.

That's what the poor widow at the temple did. She gave, not 10% but 100%. Not what was required, but in proportion to her heart desire. It was all she had to live on. Folded up inside a tattered cloth or kept inside a small pottery jar, she liquefied her financial portfolio, donating it all to the temple treasury. Now she had nothing. Zilch. Zero. Nil. Her purse was now hollow, drained of what little resources she previously called her own.

But according to Jesus, this woman had something none of those deep-pocket tithers possessed. She possessed a sacrificial spirit of worship. In her heart and mind, she was giving it all to God. In stark contrast to the "oohs" and "ahhs" others had received upon depositing their huge sums into the temple coffers, this woman's two coins hardly made a sound—much less a dent—in the collection plate. But they did make quite an impact on the heart of God's Son. But it wasn't the amount of her offering that impressed the Lord. It was the motivation and proportion of it. While others gave out of their wealth, she gave out of her poverty.

She gave her net worth, all for the sake of worship.

In her heart was no desire or expectation of recognition, and no strings were attached. She anticipated no special treatment from temple officials nor to secure for herself any favors. And there would also be no "tax deductible" benefit to her contribution.

> When you don't have very much to contribute, giving a little means a lot. Money is a relative thing. It's all a matter of perspective, really.

Some may wonder if this was a wise thing for her to do. Was she being a good steward of her resources? Would a Christian financial counselor have advised her to make such an offering? Wouldn't she risk becoming destitute and live on the streets? Would she now have to resort to begging? We're not sure. However, what is apparent is that all those risks were outweighed by the spiritual compulsion to worship through giving.

So what do her actions tell us about the condition of her heart? About her perspective on money and material possessions? About her view of God? I think you know.

By giving all she had, this widow was left now with no resources. She would have to depend solely and completely on the very God to whom she had given her last thin bit of money. She now had nothing but God. But is that such a bad place to be?

However, though she had completely emptied her purse, her heart nevertheless was now full. Full of joy. Full of hope. Full of Him! Her investment was not just in coin, but rather in kingdom. She simply believed Jehovah was worth her great sacrifice. And with just two little "mites," she became "mighty" in her worship.

## Miracle on a Mountainside

The Son of God traveled on foot, not in a custom-designed tour bus or private jet. He had no trainers, makeup artists or agents. There was no ad campaign announcing His upcoming arrival. Of course, word did spread from town to town and village to village about the Healer. But unless you had seen Him before with your own eyes, Jesus may as well have been an urban legend to you. With so many teachers and self-proclaimed prophets wandering around first-century Palestine, the stories about Jesus could have been fabricated or embellished, had they not been accompanied by so many eyewitnesses. But as the Lord's notoriety grew, so did the crowds who followed Him. In fact, it was often difficult for Him to enter even a small town due to the huge throngs of people constantly pressing in on Him.[54]

In one such encounter, Jesus is surrounded by thousands. It happened shortly after His cousin and friend, John the Baptist, had been beheaded by Herod. John had the guts to tell the king he was in sin for marrying his brother's wife. His "non-seeker-friendly" approach to evangelism landed him in the dungeon. Without any first amendment protection, he was executed, whereupon Herod was presented the bloody Baptist's head on a platter.[55] Jesus hears of John's death and seeks a private place to pray and grieve. And though He got into a boat to escape the crowds, the solitude He seeks escapes Him. With thousands following on foot to see what miraculous sign He would perform next, they eventually figure out where He is. Soon it came time to eat, and there wasn't a restaurant around for miles. So Jesus turns to one of His disciples, Phillip, and asks him a question.

> "Where shall we buy bread for these people to eat?"
>
> He asked this only to test him, for he already had in mind what he was going to do. Philip answered him, "Eight months' wages would not buy enough bread for each one to have a bite!" (John 6:5–7)

Now Philip isn't blind or dumb. He can see and he can count. Scanning the huge crowd assembled on the hillside that day, he calculates the size of the multitude, informing Jesus that their ministry budget is a bit shy of covering the cost of this late lunch. Try to picture what the disciples are facing. They had never fed 5,000 famished men before. Throw in another 10–15,000 women and children, and that brings the total between 15-20,000 for dinner![56]

It's a huge mass of people, bigger than most cities at the time. So you might imagine Philip's comments are laced with a drop of cynicism. At this point, he's probably fed up with all the peasants, thrill-seekers, sick people and fans constantly showing up out of nowhere. He's ready to enjoy some privacy for a change. The disciples even suggest that Jesus "send the crowds away, so they can go to the villages and buy themselves some food."[57] The "every man for himself" mentality. The disciples' mercy was flowing like a river, wasn't it?

Then another of his disciples, Andrew, Simon Peter's brother, spoke up, "Here is a boy with five small barley loaves and two small fish, but how far will they go among so many?" (John 6:8–9)

At least Andrew is trying! But did you ever wonder where in the world this boy came from? Obviously, he was a part of the crowd that day, but what was his story? We're not told. He may have been about 10 years old, and given the natural curiosity level of little boys, was probably darting in and out of the crowd trying to get an up-close glimpse of the action. Can't you see him nipping at the disciples' heels, no doubt irritating them with his persistent questions?

"Hey, watcha doing? Where's Jesus? Can I see Him? Is He gonna do another miracle? What's your name? I'm Timothy. My dad is a fisherman. Are you a fisherman? I'm 10 years old. How old are you? Do you have any boys in your house? My dad owns a boat. Hey, watcha doing…?"

Can you see him, with wild-eyed wonder watching the Son of God transform lives with a single touch? Perhaps he was fishing with his dad by the Sea of Galilee that day when they heard the buzz of the crowd approaching. His job may have been to hold onto the fish his father had caught. The five loaves may have even been their food for the day.

But regardless of what we *don't* know about him, we do know he ends up hanging out with Jesus' disciples and, most likely, eves dropping on their dialogue with the Master. And what he hears has the future apostles brainstorming, scratching their heads, searching for a solution to the problem of catering a take-out lunch for some 15-20,000 people. Can't you hear his pre-pubescent, enthusiastic voice bursting into the discussion?

"I have some food!"

Suddenly, the conversation grinds to a screeching halt. Turning to look, they see a kid holding up his stinky, scrawny catch. In his other hand are some hard loaves of bread. This lad's small, yet sacrificial contribution gives Philip and his cohorts a glimmer of hope. Bringing the miniscule portion of food to Jesus, the disciples listened as the Lord gave instruction for the people to sit down in the grass. You can assume the little boy sat as well, watching with rapt attention to see what Jesus would do with his small gift of worship. Perhaps his father joins him there on the grass. Then Jesus takes the few small loaves of bread and two scrawny fish and gives thanks to God. Scripture tells us what happens next:

> Jesus "distributed (the bread) to those who were seated as much as they wanted. He did the same with the fish. When they had all had enough to eat, he said to his disciples, 'Gather the pieces that are left over. Let nothing be wasted.' So they gathered them

and filled twelve baskets with the pieces of the five barley loaves left over by those who had eaten." (John 6:11–13)

This boy could not possibly have known Jesus was going to perform this miracle. He also didn't know whether anyone else had food to contribute. But it wouldn't have mattered anyway. He was only focused on what *he* had to give. Not a part of it. Not a "tithe" of it. Not what he could spare out of it. But…

…*all* of it.

His offering was small, dried up and crusty. And it likely smelled—dead fish have been known to do that. But it wasn't the size or quality of what he offered Christ that mattered. It wasn't how fresh or new it was that made a difference to Jesus. It was what it represented to the little boy that made it significant. It was his food. His sustenance. It was what a poor lad's body required to live for the day. There were no freezers back home full of deer and duck meat. There were no walk-in pantries lined with canned goods. For this peasant boy and his family, those few loaves and fish comprised what was likely their "daily bread." He was carrying his portable "cupboard" with him. And now that he had given it all away, he looks down and sees his pouch is empty. All that remains are a few scattered crumbs at the bottom—can you see them?—and the lingering odor of fish—can you smell it? There is nothing left. He gave all he had to Jesus. And what's left behind is the fulfillment and joy that comes from giving to the Lord. His offering wasn't much compared to what you or I can give, but it was his own little act of worship. By sacrificing what he had, he was saying, "Jesus, You are worth all I have to give."

> It wasn't the size or quality of what he offered Christ that mattered. It wasn't how fresh or new it was that made a difference to Jesus. It was what it represented to the little boy that made it significant.

And make note of what Christ does with his tiny investment. Every man, woman, boy and girl there that day was fully fed and satisfied. Twelve full baskets of bread were left over. Not a single soul went home hungry. All were filled, their hunger pains obliterated by the Son of God.

Better than an all-you-can-eat buffet, Jesus' miracle on the mountainside truly filled their bellies. They pushed back from the table, unable to eat another bite. Jesus had given them exactly what they needed, what they longed for. They needed something only He could provide, and He didn't disappoint.

In reality, Jesus really didn't need the little boy's fish and bread to perform this miracle. He had spoken the universe into being simply by commanding it to exist, having formed the world by His own word (Genesis 1:1; John 1:1–3). He had created everything there is out of nothing. All He needed to make the universe was Himself. With His infinite power, it boggles the mind to consider that He can do anything as easily as He does. Speak a solar system into existence. Navigate the downward path of a falling leaf. Multiply bread. Raise the dead. Heal the sick. Transform water into wine. Restore a leper. Make a blind man see. Make a lame man walk. Turn fish into more fish. Change a life. Change your life. One is no more difficult than the other for the One with infinite power.

Although He didn't require the boy's scrawny fish and hard bread, He used them anyway. And that's part of the mystery, isn't it? Though He needs nothing from us, He still graciously receives what we have to offer, no matter how pitiful, transforming it and using it for His glory. Regardless of how paltry or priceless, it's what our sacrifice represents that really matters to Him. It was a spur of the moment thing since this boy hadn't previously known about this great need. He just heard then responded. He saw the contribution he could make, and so he just did something about it. He didn't pray or wait until he sensed a "peace" about it. There was merely something inside this little guy that just said, "Do it! Go ahead. Give it to Jesus!" Some adults might question the wisdom of giving all you have on a seemingly impulsive whim like this.

Maybe you would write it off as boyish immaturity or foolishness. But there are times in life when you simply see a need and immediately a desire springs up inside you to do something about it. And while your contribution may not seem grand or significant compared to the overall need, it's still big to you.

And you may not see that God has plans for your small, yet sacrificial gift. That missionary family you housed, they went back to the field fully rejuvenated and inspired by their restful stay and time getting to know you. Your gift to that ministry came at just the right time, enabling it to continue doing God's work for another month. Those college students you had over for a cookout never forgot the touch and taste of home you provided them. That van full of junior high school students you chauffeured to the retreat included an eighth-grade girl from a broken home who was searching for an identity and a friend. She watched you that weekend, curious to see someone older than her being fun and loving. While there, she made a private but powerful decision to live for Christ. That was ten years go. She's 24 now and more passionate for God than ever, thanks in part, to you and your two fish.

In every life, God takes our small sacrifices and multiplies them. Why? Because He can, of course. But that's not all. He does it because it pleases Him when you demonstrate how worthy He is of your sacrifice. To honor Him in this way moves His heart to honor you as well, and He delights in doing something great with what you gave Him.

> God takes our small sacrifices and multiplies them. He does it because it pleases Him when you demonstrate how worthy He is of your sacrifice. To honor Him in this way moves His heart to honor you as well, and He delights in doing something great with what you gave Him.

So when the opportunity presents itself, will you be ready to make your sacrifice? When He asks you to look at your checkbook, refrigerator, calendar, talent, time, or heart, will you gladly reach in and give what you have? Will you do it on a moment's notice? Will you drop your last two coins in the box? Will you retrieve the bread and fish, gladly handing it over to Him?

Do it and then watch what the Master can do.

Like this little boy, no sacrifice you make ever goes unnoticed by Jesus. Perhaps your tiny act of worship will also inspire a miracle, influencing and satisfying thousands of hungry lives. Odds are it already has. And of the thousands there that day, like this lad, you will become the most satisfied of them all.

CHAPTER 8

# Unplugged
## Simple Worship

> Our life is frittered away by detail...Simplify, simplify!
> – Henry David Thoreau

You would have to be an alien from another solar system not to know the name Nike. As a colossal force in the world of sports gear and apparel, the name alone says it all. Today, you can explore the remote mountains of Peru or the jungles of Papua New Guinea and find local tribes who don't know about the Internet, but who are wearing Nike t-shirts. Like Coke, the Nike brand has touched virtually every place on the planet. But what you may not know is that the world-famous *swoosh* logo was created way back in 1971. Company founder Phil Knight had met a struggling young graphic design student who needed to earn some money. Knight asked the woman, Carolyn Davidson, to design a concept logo for his new company, something that would look good on the side of a shoe. Soon afterwards, Davidson produced the now familiar swoosh, for which she was paid a flat fee of $35. Many years and billions of dollars later, Carolyn's design is now the planet's most recognizable sports trademark.

But what makes the Nike swoosh so incredibly successful? And why is it so easy to remember? It's simple, that's why. Marketing gurus know the job of advertising is to pique the consumer's interest in minimum time for maximum effect. Don't waste time articulately explaining the product or giving the history of the company. Don't confuse customers with needless details. Get in there, grab their attention, and get out before they change their mind, press the remote, or turn the page. The time-tested rule still stands: Less is always more.

As Christians, we could learn a valuable lesson from the genius often found in corporate advertising.

Simplicity is also an important component of our walk with God. In the midst of all the "necessary" activities of our spiritual regimen, what often gets lost in the clutter and fog of Christianity is our actual relationship with Christ.

Once, while attending my son's t-ball game, I observed the antithesis of this principle. The stands were packed with proud parents, intently watching their little future hall-of-famers battle it out on the baseball diamond. But as typical 6-year-olds, the boys' collective attention spans lasted about as long as the run from the dugout to their respective positions. Once there, they grew bored and distracted. Their focus was on more urgent activities, like digging in the dirt, chasing butterflies or waving at grandma in the bleachers. One of those little boys, literally "out in left field," busied himself by repeatedly tossing his glove high into the air. His mother anxiously watched, silently hoping her son would snap out of his dream world and turn his attention back to the action at home plate. Finally, she couldn't stand it any longer, and her last nerve snapped. Jumping to her feet, she hurried over to the fence behind home plate, cupped her hands over her mouth and screamed,

"Tyler! Quit playing around out there! THIS IS NOT A GAME!"

The ball park suddenly went quiet as every parent's head turned and shockingly stared at the woman. The batter, whose helmet had fallen down over his eyes, became startled, pausing from his stance to look. The infield stood motionless like mannequins, their gum-chewing temporarily halted by the noise. The pitcher froze, his mouth caught in an open

Texas-sized gawk. The umpire swiveled around on his heels, intently scanning the stands with his eyes. Both coaches hung their heads, wagging them side-to-side. And just for a few seconds, everything seemed like it was in super slow-mo. Nobody moved. Finally realizing what she had actually said, this mom sheepishly cowered back to her seat, and the game resumed as if nothing had happened. The batter smacked the ball off the tee, over the shortstop's head and into left field. And Tyler responded by once more tossing his glove high into the air as the ball sped by.

What this overzealous, competitive mom had forgotten in her moment of motherly insanity was there is something even more important for a six-year-old baseball player than to catch a fly ball in left field. Of course, a time will come when little Tyler will have to grow up and take the sport—and his position—much more seriously. But what his mom didn't know was that, for now, baseball is supposed to be fun! It really *is* a game, mom! Something you "play." After all, isn't that the whole reason he signed up for the team?

Have you ever heard that mom's voice before? Not from your own mother, but from the Christian culture around you, and maybe even your own conscience. Does it sound familiar? "Hey, get busy out there! Christian life is not a game. Quit playing around! Stop enjoying yourself and get back to serving!" And unlike little Tyler, you snap back into your "doing" mode and return to work. And the whole reason you began this relationship is lost or buried alive under a mound of Christian *stuff*.

We can become so focused on the disciplines of Bible study, prayer or church activities that we forfeit our joy in the process. Because we are so intent on being the best Christians we can be, we load up our plate, thinking the more we do, the better off we are. Like the margins in our Bibles, we also fill up the margins in our lives until they become so cluttered that they leave room for little else. However, after a while, we grow weary trying to keep up the pace. It's a catch-22 because reducing such Christian activities can make us somehow feel a little less spiritual. We are told the devil never takes a vacation from his work, so neither should we. But since when has the devil become our role model?

This Christian business soon takes its toll. Before long, we experience the unthinkable. No, not falling into unmentionable sin, but something just as tragic and with equally devastating results. Our worship degenerates into a rote, mindless, even heartless activity. Unintentionally disengaging our intimacy with God through a preoccupation with Christian activities, we miss the experience with Him. We "go through the motions," failing to recognize the slow regression in our spiritual growth. We become deceived over time by a Christianity that thrives outwardly but threatens us inwardly. On the surface, no one can really notice the difference or that anything is wrong. Even we can't see it sometimes. We look as good as all the other Christians around us, so who would know, right? And beauty is lost in excessiveness. We mistakenly thought godliness meant "Christianizing" ourselves, keeping all the rules, and wearing the right "uniform." We played our position, showing up at all the games, practices, and special events while at the same time missing the one thing that really defines us as believers. That one thing is a simple and pure love for Jesus Christ.

## There's Something About Mary

Consider the woman in Scripture known as Mary of Bethany, an uncomplicated girl with natural spiritual beauty. We see her just three times in the New Testament. But interestingly, in every instance, she is found at the feet of Jesus. And each instance reveals the purity and simplicity of her relationship to Christ. Through the Gospel writer's accounts, let's look over her shoulder and try to see what she sees.

> As Jesus and his disciples were on their way, he came to a village where a woman named Martha opened her home to him. (Luke 10:38)

The village here is Bethany, located on the east side of the Mount of Olives, less than two miles from Jerusalem. The house they entered belonged to Martha, most likely Mary's older sister. The first thing we notice about these two sisters is they are very different from each other. They have contrasting personalities, which caused them to value and enjoy different things. And that's okay. God made them that way. Perhaps you can identify because you're very different from your sister or brother. Maybe you thank God every day that you are! But those differences can be the very things that complement your relationship with your siblings. They may have driven you over the edge at times! Siblings are like that, you know. One is messy while the other is a neat freak. One is outgoing and gregarious while the other is quiet and contemplative. One is athletic and the other is musical. One is organized and calculated while the other is carefree and spontaneous. You may have even been tempted to provide your brother or sister with a one-way ticket to Heaven. But in spite of conflicts and contrasts, you lived to tell the story.

You can then likely appreciate Mary and Martha's sibling rivalry, identifying with one or the other. Martha is a typical "doer." A planner and list-maker, she does things by the book. Task-oriented, she is energized by being effective and efficient. In short, she gets stuff done. Checklist in hand, she is organized to the max. Administrative. Competent. Resourceful. Nothing wasted. She cleans the house before guests arrive, even in places they'll never see. She is capable, proficient, and professional. Of course, all these are admirable qualities. Everyone should strive for excellence in these areas since some of the world's most successful people are "Marthas." Without people like her, the world—and the church—would be a real mess.

And then there's Mary.

> We mistakenly miss the one thing that really defines us as believers. That one thing is a simple and pure love for Jesus Christ.

Probably the younger sister, Mary is already at a certain disadvantage with respect to her older sister. She is not the task-oriented person Martha is. She doesn't default to household chores like her sister. She doesn't wake up early in the morning thinking about all the things she has to do that day. There is no "to-do" list for her. That would stifle her creativity. She is more free-spirited and spontaneous. She isn't as much into what *has* to be done as she is what she *gets* to do. She prefers people to programs. Talking over tasks. Devotion over duty. Relationships over regimen. Wherever the action and excitement are, that's where you'll find Mary. She bores easily but gets energized when around people. She'd rather spend an evening watching a movie than painting the kitchen cabinets. Having a party is more important than rearranging the living room furniture. Mary is happy when folks are together while Martha is most content when her world is in order. Martha's motto is "Let's get it done." Mary's is "Let's hang out or do something fun!"

Again, one is not bad and the other good. But as you might guess, their differences may have created a little conflict at times. And Jesus highlights one of those conflicts in this passage.

*(Martha) had a sister called Mary, who sat at the Lord's feet listening to what he said. But Martha was distracted by all the preparations that had to be made. She came to him and asked, "Lord, don't you care that my sister has left me to do the work by myself? Tell her to help me!" "Martha, Martha," the Lord answered, "you are worried and upset about many things, but only one thing is needed. Mary has chosen what is better, and it will not be taken away from her."* (Luke 10:39–42)

Jesus comes to their home, and naturally both sisters respond in opposite ways. Martha is preparing and working while Mary is sitting on the floor listening. Mary must have been thinking, "Why isn't Martha in here with the Lord? C'mon, it is the greatest possible honor to sit at His feet and hear Him teach us. Why worry about cooking more food at a time like this? She is really missing out on a great experience."

> "I know how much You love a good work ethic. I've read what You said about the sluggard in Proverbs, and I am obeying You by doing something special for You."

Meanwhile, Martha is stewing in the kitchen, "Why isn't Mary in here with me preparing for the Lord? C'mon, this is the greatest possible honor to be able to serve the Lord in this way. Why just sit there like a lazy person at a time like this? She is definitely not in God's will."

However, Martha takes her thoughts a step further, marching into the living room and telling Jesus to get Mary in gear.

It's as if Martha is saying, "The work! The work, Lord! See how I'm serving you? I know how much You love a good work ethic. I've read what You said about the sluggard in Proverbs, and I am obeying You by doing something special for You. And all by myself now that Mary has left the kitchen. I'm standing alone for what is right, just like Esther and Daniel and all the others who were truly committed to You. Now Mary, on the other hand, is more like the lazy, unbelieving generation that wandered in the desert for 40 years, unwilling to obey You. But here am I, ready to do Your will, Lord. I have tried to tell her that she's going to be in big trouble if she doesn't start showing more fruit in her life. You know, come to think of it, maybe she's not really saved, after all. Anyway, would You just tell her to get back to serving?"

Of course, we really don't know exactly what Martha was thinking, though Jesus does say "many things" were bothering her. It is fairly safe to say that her preference of work over waiting in the Lord's presence caused her to be upset and angry with her sister. The problem is, in the original Greek text, the verse indicates Mary had already been in the kitchen helping and preparing. But in Martha's mind, it just wasn't "enough."

With some people it's never enough, is it? Now, let's be fair to Martha and cut her some slack for a minute. The Lord may have dropped in unexpectedly at their house. Martha wasn't prepared for such a visit, and it threw her world into a tailspin to think that the Son of God might see her dirty dishes and unswept floor. Besides, a visit from the Messiah may not have been on her itinerary for the day. It hadn't made the "to do" list. She wanted to give Jesus her very best. And because of His unexpected arrival, she would have to take some emergency measures that would require everyone pitching in to help. But thanks to Mary's "laziness," Martha's already high-stress level was peaking, turning her anxiety into anger. Jesus, knowing all things, understood what Martha was experiencing and corrects her with a loving yet firm response.

Martha was worried, upset, and stressed out. And in need of a life lesson from Christ. Now the flip side is Mary's perspective. She is peaceful and content. And while there was nothing wrong with preparing a meal for Jesus, the Lord is clearly saying there's something "better." The Lord isn't suggesting we all sit cross-legged on the floor and read our Bibles 24/7. This is not a justification for living as a recluse or not working hard at school, on the job, or in ministry. But what He is saying is there is something He values even more than doing stuff for Him. The only thing we really need, the only real requirement, according to Christ, is to simply be with Him. Boiling it all down to the bare essentials, Jesus values "one thing" above all others.

*Being* over *doing*.

Not that we shouldn't *do*. It's just that there is something greater. It's not as visible or tangible or measurable as doing and serving.

But it is *better*.

Jesus is saying, "Martha, you are complicating things here. There is something I want more than your food and service right now. I want your fellowship."

Christ isn't being petty here. Nor is He playing favorites. He's just being consistent with His heart. He is expressing a desire and truth He echoes elsewhere in Scripture. He chose us so we would *be with Him*—now and forever. It is a theme often repeated during Jesus' ministry, as well as elsewhere in the New Testament.[58]

Mary was on to something here. She chose the feet of Jesus to be her "place." She had discovered the "secret," the "one thing" God desires. Simple worship in His presence. Uncomplicated. Uncluttered. Basic. Natural. Pure. Childlike. And why is this so important? For at least two reasons. First, it helps us focus on our relationship with the Person of Christ. Doing the work of Jesus can never substitute for knowing the Person of Jesus. We don't worship an organization, a faith, the family, the church, or even the Bible. We worship a Person. And when He is in the central spotlight of our lives, it delights His heart like nothing else! After all, that's why we were made. Second, this simple and pure devotion to Christ rescues us from the danger of falling prey to religious ritual or even accepting another gospel. This was one of Paul's many concerns for the Corinthian Christians.

> *For I am jealous for you with a godly jealousy; for I betrothed you to one husband, that to Christ I might present you as a pure virgin. But I am afraid, lest as the serpent deceived Eve by his craftiness, your minds should be led astray from the* simplicity and purity of devotion *to Christ.* (2 Corinthians 11:2–4)

So here's Mary, just glad to be there...with Jesus. Listening to His Word. And as she hears His words, she also sees His heart. There is no other way to describe it. She is captivated by the Person of Jesus. While in His presence, she forgets everything else that may trouble her. Nothing else really matters. She is with Him.

And she is satisfied.

Got any clutter in your life that needs to be pushed aside for a higher priority? Have you become unbalanced in your life, placing too much time and energy on serving? Will you pause and worship at His feet, listening for Him to speak to you? And above all else, are you still captivated by the Person of Christ?

## Dead Man Walking

The next time we see Mary, we find her once again at the feet of Jesus. However, this occasion is not as casual and carefree. Life has taken a more serious tone. Lazarus, the brother of Mary and Martha, has died, having been very sick. Word is sent to Jesus, who is in another town miles away. Strangely, He waits several days before going to Bethany. Upon His arrival, Lazarus has been entombed for four days. A huge wake is still in progress, with many friends and mourners expressing their condolences. A heavy cloud of grief now covers the little home where Jesus once dined. However, before He ever reaches Bethany, Martha hears He is on His way and goes out to meet Him. She has no interest in preparing a meal for Him this time. Far greater than her need to serve is her heart's need to be with Him. Martha has learned her lesson. She understands what that "one thing" is now. Her priorities are in order. Having traded her kitchen apron for a mourning shawl, she runs to Him.

> Doing the work of Jesus can never substitute for knowing the Person of Jesus. We don't worship an organization, a faith, the family, the church, or even the Bible. We worship a Person.

> "Lord," Martha said to Jesus, "if you had been here, my brother would not have died. But I know that even now God will give you whatever you ask."
>
> Jesus said to her, "Your brother will rise again."
>
> Martha answered, "I know he will rise again in the resurrection at the last day."

Jesus said to her, "I am the resurrection and the life. He who believes in me will live, even though he dies; and whoever lives and believes in me will never die. Do you believe this?"

"Yes, Lord," she told him, "I believe that you are the Christ, the Son of God, who was to come into the world." (John 11:21–27)

Confessing her belief in Jesus as the Messiah and Savior, she also declares her faith in Him as the Son of God. Though she may not have yet pieced together the truth and mystery of the Trinity, she nevertheless knew Jesus was divine. Martha finally discovered what her baby sister had experienced. This family tragedy caused her to pause and look into the face of Jesus. And she was captivated with what she saw.

Jesus then asks her to go get Mary. Upon hearing the Master is calling for her, Mary rises quickly and sprints to meet Him. Her friends think she is heading out to the tomb, so they follow her.

Seeing her Savior, Mary peers through a haze of tears until she spots the throng surrounding Jesus. As you might imagine, her grief has robbed her of rest. She is exhausted, weary from four days of wailing over her lost brother. Upon reaching Jesus, she falls at His feet, repeating word-for-word what her sister had said, "Lord, if you had been here, my brother would not have died" (John 11:32).

Apparently, these two sisters have something in common after all! I can picture Jesus pausing to look around. He sees the mourners who have accompanied Mary. Then He gazes down at His friend, who is still weeping at His feet. But Christ sees beyond her tears. He peers deep into her heart to see the pain, grief, and the darkness of the soul she and her sister were experiencing. And He understands it all. It becomes obvious that Jesus loved this family very much (John 11:3,5). The sisters' sorrow gripped His spirit, deeply moving Him within. Inquiring as to where Lazarus' tomb was, they begin the short journey to the graveyard. Jesus walks to the tomb, perhaps holding up Mary under one arm. This is now the second funeral procession this week for Mary. And the crowd this time is surely larger due to Jesus' presence. It's a sad day in Bethany.

> Does the Savior you worship weep with you when you hurt?

Jesus wept.

Two words. One in the Greek. An amazing phenomenon, but not just because tears flowed from the Carpenter's eyes. He had been moved like this before when encountering a poor leper (Mark 1:41). And He would later weep over Jerusalem (Luke 19:41). But this time Jesus wasn't weeping over them. He was crying with them. A wave of emotion swept over the Son of God. His eyes filled with tears, brimming to the edge then spilling over, flowing down His brown cheeks and into His beard. Jesus was crying, so much so that He was noticeably and visibly moved, for those standing there that day commented on how much He must have loved Lazarus (John 11:36). And upon reaching the tomb, another wave of emotion hit Him and He wept again.

Does the Savior you worship weep with you when you hurt?

It wouldn't hurt us to be a little more like Mary here. Her view of God enabled her to approach Him and fall at His feet at any time and for any reason, especially when confused and crushed by the knockout punches life throws at us.

Jesus then gives orders for the stone to be rolled away from the tomb. Martha expresses her concern to the Lord that this might be a bad idea considering the stench of the rotting corpse. Lazarus had assumed room temperature four days ago, and just might part the crowd with his ensuing smell. Jesus responds by basically saying, "Trust Me here." Then He gave instructions for the stone to be removed from the tomb.

Now we can only speculate about what might have been going on in Heaven around that time and the potential conversation between God and Lazarus. Imagine the following dialogue.

God: Lazarus, come here, son. I have something I want you to do.

Lazarus: Yes, Lord. Here I am. What can I do for You? Name it, Father. Anything.

God: I want you to go back to earth for Me.

Lazarus: (surprised look on his face) G-g-go back to earth? You mean, leave this beautiful place and return to that sinful planet down there? Why, Lord? Did I do something wrong?

God: No. You did nothing wrong, Lazarus. I am sending you back down on a very special mission for Me. Because of your miraculous return, you will restore hope and healing to your family. But beyond this, you will glorify My Son by inspiring faith in thousands. Then, after what will seem like a moment, you will come back to Me. And we will all be together forever.

Lazarus: Yes, Father. Of course, I will be glad to do that. I will do anything that causes others to glory in Your Son. When do I leave?

God: Shh. Listen. He is calling for you now.

Jesus called in a loud voice, "Lazarus, come out!" (John 11:43)

Theologians have speculated that had Jesus not specifically used Lazarus' name, every dead person in that graveyard would have come back to life. Perhaps. But more important is He commanded a validated corpse to come back from the dead! And out comes Lazarus, bound head to toe in strips of linen. Hopping out of the grave—or at least taking very small steps. He is unwrapped and let go, smelling as sweet as Spring. No doubt the first thing he feels is the loving embrace of his sisters. Mary and Martha are crying once again, but for a different reason this time. Chances are, watching that reunion moved Jesus to shed more tears. And what happens next must have put a smile on Lazarus' face.

Therefore many of the Jews who had come to visit Mary, and had seen what Jesus did, put their faith in him. (John 11:45)

Mission accomplished, Lazarus.

As for Mary, there was something about her worship that enabled her to trust Christ to do something great for her. Hers was a childlike innocence. She knew that because Jesus was there, somehow everything would be alright.

What about you? Will you worship at His feet, trusting Him to do something amazing for you? Is there some great need you have that only He can meet? Will you worship at His feet until He rolls away the stone?

## The Smell of Worship

The last time we see Mary in Scripture it's no surprise we find her once again at Jesus' feet. When we first met her worshiping at His feet, she was sitting there because she wanted to *know* Him (Luke 10:38–42). Then we see her caught up in the embrace of worship because of her desire to *believe* in Him (John 11:31–32). Lastly, we last see Mary anointing His feet out of devotion to *honor* Him (John 12:1–8). Each is a beautiful act of worship, but perhaps this third scene is more compelling than all the rest.

It's Wednesday, just two days before Jesus is crucified. Simon the Leper gives a party, presumably in Jesus' honor.[59] Lazarus is also there, along with his sisters, Mary and Martha, and the disciples. Can you even conceive what such a gathering must have been like? Jesus is having dinner with people whose lives He has forever changed. There's James and John, the former "Sons of Thunder." Confrontational, aggressive, and perhaps even prone to violence, they were changed through meeting Messiah.[60] James became the first apostle to die for Him.[61] John would forever become known as the "apostle of love."

Then there's Simon the Zealot. He used to be a political assassin, a type of first-century terrorist. Talk about a life changing! Of course, the other Simon there used to have leprosy, and Lazarus used to be dead! They were all a bunch of "used-to-be's." And if you think about it, so are we.

Paul reminds us:

> Do you not know that the wicked will not inherit the kingdom of God? Do not be deceived: Neither the sexually immoral nor idolaters nor adulterers nor male prostitutes nor homosexual of-

fenders nor thieves nor the greedy nor drunkards nor slanderers nor swindlers will inherit the kingdom of God. *And that is what some of you were.* But you were washed, you were sanctified, you were justified in the name of the Lord Jesus Christ and by the Spirit of our God. (1 Corinthians 6:9–11)

Can you see them sharing how Jesus had saved and changed them? Perhaps they took turns around the table, with each of them telling their own story of what Jesus had done for them, of how He had made them whole and new. And each story was an anthem of praise, a verbal worship offering.[62] Martha is serving dinner (naturally), and Mary…well, Mary finds yet another way to demonstrate how worthy she thinks Jesus is. She may not have experienced a lifestyle as outwardly sinful as her spiritual brothers, but this doesn't hinder the depth of her worship as she steps forward to honor Him in her own special way. John writes:

> Do not be deceived: Neither the sexually immoral nor idolaters nor adulterers nor male prostitutes nor homosexual offenders nor thieves nor the greedy nor drunkards nor slanderers nor swindlers will inherit the kingdom of God.

Mary then took a pound of very costly perfume of pure nard, and anointed the feet of Jesus and wiped His feet with her hair; and the house was filled with the fragrance of the perfume. (John 12:3)

This expensive perfume was valued at 300 denarii, equal to about a year's wage for a rural worker.[63] Mary pours it over Jesus' head and feet. The word used to describe this perfume ("costly") is the same word used to describe the "precious" blood of Christ and the "precious" character of a godly woman (1 Peter 1:18–19, 3:4). And like those, it too was rare. She proceeds to wipe His feet with her hair, spreading the fragrance so that it fills the entire room.[64] This perfume measures about a pint and is made of pure "nard." Granted, "nard" doesn't sound very pleasant to us, but to them it was very precious. This particular perfume was imported from India and contained extracted oil from a plant native to that region. Keep in mind, there were no malls, department stores or online shopping back then. We don't know how Mary obtained the perfume or how long she had waited for it. But we can be confident that she had been saving up her money for some time. Of course, she didn't have to use this perfume on Jesus. She could have used it for her own pleasure. Instead, she chose to pour it out, *all* of it, on Jesus. It was a worship gift that represented her unique love for Him. It cost her a lot of money to show how much she loved Jesus.

But it also cost Mary her reputation. When she "undid" her hair, that was something nice Jewish women didn't do in public. In doing so, she laid her glory at His feet (1 Corinthians 11:15). The disciples began scolding her for this kind of lavish worship, objecting that the perfume should have been sold and the money given to the poor.[65] But this was a bogus protest for several reasons:

First, it was none of their business what Mary did with her money, especially concerning how she chose to give to God.

Second, we don't see any of them honoring Jesus in such a lavish manner.

Third, if Jesus wasn't correcting her, why should they?

And fourth, it was a false spirituality on Judas' part to object since he, as treasurer, used to steal money from the ministry account.[66] This thief would have stolen the proceeds from the sale of the perfume as well.

So instead of rebuking Mary, Jesus sternly reprimands His disciples. He then turns to commend Mary for her simple yet profound act of worship.

You see, Mary possessed a unique insight into the person and work of Christ. She saw something even the disciples failed to see about Him and His mission. She understood His death was approaching, and so she anointed Him for His burial. And how did she know this? Because of her simple and passionate devotion to Him. She knew "Messiah" meant "anointed one." She knew this because of all that time spent at His feet, *listening*.

Soaking in His every word, she believed what He said. And part of His teaching had been regarding His impending crucifixion. So Mary wanted to do something that would demonstrate her love for her Savior. It wasn't a forced pious act meant to impress others. It was just an overflow of her love for Him. It was a natural thing for her to do. It. Was. Simple.

But Jesus also commends Mary for recognizing the urgency of the hour. She knew the Lord wasn't always going to physically be with her, so she took advantage of the short time she had with Him. The disciples are no doubt shocked as Jesus tells them to "leave her alone." He considered what she had done to be a "beautiful thing." He then honors her by saying that wherever the Gospel is preached, what she has done would be mentioned. What a legacy!

And what did her sacrifice do? (Mark 14:6-7) It became an <u>example</u> to the disciples—a mild rebuke. It became a *fragrance* in the house (John 12:3)—filling the whole place. You can be sure that every time they smelled that brand of perfume, they thought of Mary and her worship of Jesus. But it also became an enduring *witness* to the world. Everyone now knows of her devotion to Jesus. Do they know about yours? She left her mark for Jesus. What will yours be?

To be honest, our Christian culture often labels simplicity as shallow or elementary. We prefer our worship polished, slick, structured… *planned.* Not for Mary. It wasn't a waste of time for Mary to sit at Jesus' feet. It wasn't a waste of hope to ask Him to help her dead brother. And it wasn't a waste of money to pour that perfume all over Jesus. And for Mary, her simple devotion paid off each time. That's because nothing is ever wasted when poured out on Jesus. Not your time, your money, your hope, or your "perfume."

You think Mary knows something we don't. Her worship tells us that when you are hopelessly in love with someone, you tend to lose track of time. When you're in love, you can hope against all hope, and you rarely think about cost. In light of Him, those things just don't matter (Luke 18:29–30). Jesus was "worth it" to her.

When was the last time you "blew an afternoon" on Jesus? When did you last sacrifice something precious and valuable for Him and His cause? Are you willing to risk your relationships, reputation, and even your job for Jesus Christ? Mary just wanted to be with her Lord. Is your relationship with Him like that?

## Recapturing Your Worship

I wonder if Mary would recognize our brand of Christianity today. Ever since she first sat at His feet, she was in love with Him. She just couldn't get enough of Jesus. Sometimes we act as though we've had enough of Jesus. We show up, occasionally, to get a little dose on Sunday. We rationalize we've heard it all before. We've already learned about Him, read the story, and memorized the verse. But Christ is not a collection of facts you learn. He's a Savior you know and love. Our problem is that many Christians begin with all the enthusiasm of a rabid football fan, but end up looking like zombies in line at the local DMV.

We must constantly guard against having:

- doctrine but not desire
- rules but not reasons
- religion but not relationship
- purity but not passion
- service but not simplicity
- form but not substance

You may want to take some time just to remember when, how, and why Christ saved you. Ponder what made your Christian life so vibrant and exciting in the beginning? What simple devotion did you have then that you need to return to? Who was inspiring you in your walk with Him? Do you need him again? What about time alone with God? Prayer? Obedience? Fellowship? Meditation? Worship? Ever go back to the place where you asked Christ into your life? Have you ever called the person who led you to Christ just to say "thanks" one more time? Jesus says in order to go forward, at times, you must first go back.[67]

> To be honest, our Christian culture often labels simplicity as shallow or elementary. We prefer our worship polished, slick, structured… *planned.*

So have you grown cold towards God? You may be very active for Him. But do you love Him? Better yet, are you "in love" with Him? Ask yourself the additional following questions:

Have I ever been more devoted to Christ at any other time in my life?

Has there ever been a time when I was more in love with Him than I am right now?

When was the last time I told Jesus I loved Him?

When was the last time I gave up something costly, just to demonstrate my worship of Him?

How long has it been since I stared at the cross in amazement?

How long has it been since I felt deep emotion over His love for me?

Have I ever wept over how worthy He is?

Maybe you need to meet the Savior for the first time. If so, then put down this book right now and trust Him to forgive your sins and be your Savior.

Remember the story of the little boy who was scolded for playing around in the outfield at the beginning of this chapter? Maybe we could learn something from him, too. The game of baseball wasn't complex to him. It was just fun.

Spend some time at Jesus' feet in worship.

Then go toss your glove high in the air.

Go toss your glove in the air a while.

CHAPTER 9

# It Was a God Thing
## Unexplainable Worship

If God is small enough for us to understand,
He isn't big enough for us to worship.
– Anonymous

With all we know about God, we must confess that our knowledge is still limited and finite. Like Abraham, there are times when, in reverence, we fall on our face in humility before Him. Like Job, times when we shut up and place our hand over our mouth. And like Isaiah, we gain an acute awareness of our "smallness." Though we may become educated in biblical knowledge, there is a vast ocean of truth and experience concerning God that still lies outside our present reality and experience. We assert the Lord never acts in ways contradictory to His Word, and yet we often cannot track His movements by citing a specific chapter and verse. At times, He surprises us by taking the unexpected, intangible, or untraceable path. He does many things we just don't understand, sometimes hurling a divine curveball our way if only to remind us He is God and we are not. What He told the prophet Isaiah still holds true:

> "For My thoughts are not your thoughts, neither are your ways My ways," declares the LORD.
>
> "For as the heavens are higher than the earth, So are My ways higher than your ways, And My thoughts than your thoughts. Isaiah 55:8–9

God's methods and ways intersect on a level far beyond human understanding. You may, somehow, through superior intellect or utter determination, decipher some of life's conundrums. But you will never completely understand God or unpack all His ways. In that sense, He is truly "unknowable." It is as if you come to a point in your spiritual journey where the road ends at an impassable chasm. You stand motionless, staring across a vast expanse. On the other side resides the "rest" of the knowledge of God—that part you don't, and *can't*, comprehend. Between the two sides is a sheer drop-off, leading straight down to nothingness. Your toes inch over the precipice at the point where human understanding ends. Peering into the distance, you are unable to see through the thick smoke engulfing the other side. You've officially arrived at the edge of reason and learning, a place where the credits roll, announcing the film of our knowledge has officially ended this side of Heaven. From that location, there is not much left to do but drop to your knees and worship this God who is so beyond you. *That's* the "rest" of God. And it's unexplorable territory. At least in this life. Is it any wonder Paul wrote:

> Though we may become educated in biblical knowledge, there is a vast ocean of truth and experience concerning God that still lies outside our present reality and experience.

> Oh, the depth of the riches both of the wisdom and knowledge of God! How unsearchable are His judgments and unfathomable His ways! For WHO HAS KNOWN THE MIND OF THE LORD, OR WHO BECAME HIS COUNSELOR? Or WHO HAS FIRST GIVEN TO HIM THAT IT MIGHT BE PAID BACK TO HIM AGAIN? For from Him and through Him and to Him are all things. To Him be the glory forever. Amen. Romans 11:33–36

Perhaps you've visited this place before. Maybe you've gone there often in your experience with God. Or maybe He has led you there, giving you a snapshot glance of His glory. Has God ever done that for you, bringing you to a moment that was far beyond your knowledge, expectations, and understanding? Have you ever known an instant when the only explanation for what just occurred was, "It was a God thing?" A cancerous lump disappears with no medical explanation. A fatal accident is narrowly avoided. The friend or relative you thought would never become a Christian suddenly surrenders to Jesus. A bizarre string of supernatural coincidences happens to you, leading up to a huge, unexpected benefit. You witness a service where a man preaches, an outpouring of God's grace occurs and where huge numbers respond to the Gospel. You take part in a mission trip and see the Good News of Christ taken to a place where it has never gone before. Something you thought would never happen somehow miraculously does. A desperate need is met just in the nick of time, at the very last moment. You pray, and…Bang! It happens.

Several years ago, my wife and I started a little church in our neighborhood. In preparation for this adventure, we attended a popular church planting conference, expecting to learn some wisdom. One thing we knew we needed was financial support. So, during the *five*-hour drive back home, we prayed, out loud, and for specific requests. Then I said:

"Lord, would you speak to one of Your servants today, and tell *him* to give towards this vision and ministry?"

And because I wanted God to put His unique fingerprint on this venture, I added,

"Would you specifically tell this person to 'Write Jeff the check now?'"

Two days later, a small envelope arrived in my mailbox. It was from a dear friend and woman whose daughter had been a part of my ministry years ago. A true listener, this woman is a God-seeker and prayer warrior. Her note read, "While listening to the Lord a few days ago, He told me to give you this check." And then she added, "He specifically told me to 'Write Jeff the check now!'"

Included with the note was a check for a significant sum of money to help us launch our church. Reading those words sent chills of joy and awe all over me. I shouted praise to God and couldn't wait to share the news with my wife. We both agreed it was definitely a *God Thing*, and further confirmation we were to move forward with starting this ministry.

There is an element to moments like these that is both mystical and mysterious. They are occurrences that cannot be brushed aside by mere coincidence. No, there is only one explanation for them . . . GOD. He unmistakably did something for you. He *showed up!*

But lest we become too preoccupied with the spectacular, we must recognize that these "God-moments" are not limited to blatantly supernatural interventions. They can also come in the quiet solitude of our soul. Like lying in a sleeping bag under a cool, cloudless Colorado night sky. Galaxy-gazing on your back with crystal clear vision, the stars are crisp, almost touchable, brighter than ever before against a velvet backdrop. You stare into space, spotting clusters and constellations you've never seen before. And in the chill of the Rocky Mountain air, you lock-on like a laser-guided missile to the wonder of it all. God is spreading His canopy for you, showing you but a tiny fraction of His grandeur.

Or maybe it comes to you through witnessing the birth of a child, capturing with your mind's camera the indelible image of a newborn taking its first-ever breath of earth's air. The miracle of new life captivates you, and the only explanation is the Creator. Or perhaps in the midst of a difficult time, such as a severe personal loss or deep depression, you hear Him whisper softly, "I'm still here. I still love you." It's a voice only your spirit can discern, intended for your benefit alone.[68]

It is during those times that God parts the curtain of the normal for a brief instant, just for you. You see God in a way you have never seen Him before. Your perception of Him and perspective of things changes. He's "bigger," more awesome, and personal than you had ever realized. And it is for events such as these that a special kind of worship is in order. It's worship inspired by the unexplainable, and one reminding you He alone is God.

Can you recall events, spiritual experiences, or moments of biblical enlightenment that have marked you? These indelible impressions are like tattoos imprinted deep within your soul.

Scripture is full of such moments. Essentially, all of Scripture is a "God-Moment," a 1,500-year timespan filled with incredible, unexplainable accounts when the Creator chose to crash the party. Each one occurred for a specific purpose, sometimes on behalf of a person, family or even a nation's benefit. And each one revealed something about Him as well, subsequently inspiring a response of worship.

Let's consider three scenes in biblical history when this happened.

## Scene One: Angels Watching Over Us

Israel finds herself greatly disadvantaged in a war against a formidable Assyrian enemy that is camped outside Jerusalem. In a matter of hours, this pagan army will almost certainly level the Jewish capital city and turn it into a parking lot. But the good news for Israel is that God had promised He would not let that happen, vowing, "I will defend this city to save it for My own sake and for My servant David's sake."[69] Tension mounts as the evening falls on Palestine. And while the soldiers of Israel are making sure their last wills and testaments are in order, their Assyrian counterparts are settling in for a good night's sleep. Of course, the Jewish people had reason to be a little nervous. Traditionally, those whom the Assyrians didn't kill, they conquered, often leading the defeated away by tying ropes to rings bored through their noses. Assyria had laid waste to all other enemies, and as such, they were a dreaded foe. Plus, they were undefeated coming into this contest.

But that night, God decides to give Israel and Assyria a memory neither will soon forget. For Israel, this will be one for the highlight reel—a scene soon to find it's way into the national archives. That very night, God sends "the angel of the Lord," who promptly slaughters 185,000 Assyrian soldiers while they slept.[70] Having gone to bed confident and cocky, they wake up very dead. And how did He slaughter such a mass of military in such a short time? As documented in secular records, Greek historian Herodotus suggested their destruction was the result of a fast-acting plague of some sort, brought on by mice or rats. Others suggest it had to do with bad food, in which case they should definitely fire the camp cook. If true, this deadly, coincidental illness was great timing for Israel because she was about to be destroyed.

> Lest we become too preoccupied with the spectacular, we must recognize that "God-moments" are not limited to blatantly supernatural interventions. They can also come in the quiet solitude of our soul.

But regardless of the method employed, the truth is this was a supernatural slaughter. Pleasant? No. Gruesome. Yes. Smelly? Most definitely, especially as the 185,000 bodies began to bloat and decompose in the hot sun. Yahweh's timing and judgment arrived in a way that unmistakably declared, "God was here." Of course, if you're Assyria's King Sennacherib, this is a definitive, defeating blow to your invasion plans. So he did what any king with half a brain would do—he packed up and went home. But his bad fortune got even worse when he got there. While worshiping his god, his sons promptly came in and murdered him.[71]

Israel, on the other hand, now had a tangible and visible reason to believe the Lord was on her side. God was out destroying their enemies while they were sleeping and snoring. That ought to inspire some real worship, don't you think? Surely the soldiers and citizens of Israel didn't yawn at this miracle. This was a God-moment for the purpose of Israel's' protection and survival.

## Scene Two: Rebel Forces Go South

Rewind several hundred years. Moses has led the people of God out of Egypt through an incredible series of supernatural events popularly known as the "Ten Plagues." Talk about some God-Moments! These lessons to a hardened Pharaoh are some of the most vivid, painful, and interactive audio-visual aids ever experienced by mankind. But in spite of these lessons and others, such as a pillar of fire and miraculous manna food from Heaven, some of those redeemed out of bondage still failed to get the point, refusing to obey God. They thought they had a better plan than His messenger had revealed. One of these "Einsteins" was a man named Korah. Grumpy and discontent, he began a nationwide campaign against Moses. His basic gripe went something like this:

> "Moses, You think you're hot stuff, don't you? You're so 'high and mighty,' you and that stick of yours, not to mention your wimpy little brother. Well, you're no better than any one of us. Besides, where is this new land you promised us? All I see is desert and sand. In case you haven't noticed, nothing grows in sand. We were better off back in Egypt! So you can go back up on that mountain and play God all you want, but just leave us out of it. We're going back home!"

So persuasive was Korah that he convinced 250 influential leaders to follow his rebellion. Little did he know that Moses never aspired to control the people. He simply wanted to serve and obey God. Unfortunately, Korah's heart was also hardened, and this uprising would have to be dealt with quickly and decisively. Moses' response to this attempted coup-d'état was to inform all of Israel to stand back from the tents of Korah and his merry band of malcontents. Then Moses responds to their allegations, declaring to the people:

"By this you shall know that the Lord has sent me to do all these deeds; for this is not my doing. If these men die the death of all men or if they suffer the fate of all men, *then* the Lord has not sent me. But if the Lord brings about an entirely new thing and the ground opens its mouth and swallows them up with all that is theirs, and they descend alive into Sheol, then you will understand that these men have spurned the Lord" (Numbers 16:28–30).

But before Korah can protest or offer a slightly less deadly "if-then scenario," God shows up in a big way.

> As he finished speaking all these words, the ground that was under them split open; and the earth opened its mouth and swallowed them up, and their households, and all the men who belonged to Korah with their possessions. So they and all that belonged to them went down alive to Sheol; and the earth closed over them, and they perished from the midst of the assembly. All Israel who were around them fled at their outcry, for they said, "The earth may swallow us up!" Fire also came forth from the Lord and consumed the two hundred and fifty men who were offering the incense. (Numbers 16:31–35)

Okay, there's a little bit of mass hysteria going on here among the Israelites. And can you blame them? The earth just split apart, swallowing a large group of their friends while fire was shooting out of the Tabernacle, killing another 250 of them! You can be sure the image of those rebels sliding into the netherworld was indelibly imprinted on their minds for a long time. And yet, even with this clear display of God's judgment, the people refused to acknowledge God or bow down to worship Him. Amazingly, the very next day after witnessing this terrifying scene, another complaint rose against Moses. "You killed the Lord's people," they said. This second rebellion prompted the Lord to show up in a cloud, telling Moses to "Get away from among this congregation, that I may consume them in a moment" (Numbers 16:45). God was visibly angry because the people had stubbornly resisted His plan and provision. They had learned nothing from the example of Korah. His terrible judgment was about to fall on a few hundred thousand of them when Moses and Aaron fell on their faces before God in worship and intercession for the people. By the time Aaron had made atonement, 14,700 had already died from an awful plague.

Here was a God-moment given for the purpose of judgment of God's people. Eventually, they would learn to approach God with fear and reverence and submit to His chosen leaders (Numbers 17:12–13).

## Scene Three: Will the Real God Please Show Up?

In this unforgettable episode, the prophet Elijah made a gutsy and dangerous decision. He has confronted evil King Ahab of Israel concerning his worship of false gods. As you might expect, the king did not appreciate Elijah's critique of his religion one bit. People hate it when you criticize their religion, especially when you claim your religion is the only way. But Elijah had to confront the king because he was supposed to be spiritually leading Israel into God's ways instead of leading her into apostasy. So Elijah makes a proposal to Ahab. One that will settle the matter of "Who is God?" once and for all. He pitches the idea of having a contest between the two deities on Mount Carmel. "And just to sweeten the pot a bit," Elijah offers, "you can bring 450 prophets of Baal and 400 prophets of Asherah. I alone will represent Yahweh."

So King Ahab, thinking this would be a cakewalk, bought into the idea. Word spread about the event, and on the morning of game day, thousands came to see which god would take home the championship trophy. To make things fair and to create a level playing field, both Elijah and the prophets of Baal get to lay an ox on an altar of wood. Then they would have the opportunity to call on their respective gods to see who would answer. The god who responds with fire will prove himself to be the real god. And everyone present thought this was a good idea since both parties believed their god to be responsible for thunder, lighting and storms. The prophets of Baal won the coin toss, and so they went first.

Taking their place center stage at the altar, they began to pray, "O Baal, answer us. O Baal, answer us." But there was no reply. So they prayed a little louder, but they were only met by silence. "Hmm. Perhaps Baal prefers more movement and drama," they may have concluded. So they began leaping wildly around the altar. Still no answer. This went on for several hours until about lunchtime. Elijah, who had been watching all this and possibly covering a slight smirk on his face, began mocking the prophets.

"Cry aloud, for he is a god; either he is meditating, occupied or gone aside, he is busy or he is on a journey, or perhaps he is sleeping and must be awakened."[72]

Talk about sarcasm! Elijah is breaking every imaginable law of political correctness here. In the original Hebrew, the phrase "he is busy" can mean "gone to relieve himself." Elijah is saying, "Hey, maybe your god is gone to the bathroom. In that case, you better knock harder on the door." Can't you hear his cynicism? "Oh, boys, maybe Baal is gone on a vacation. Maybe you should leave him a voice mail and call it a day, huh?"

Elijah's mocking only heightened the Baal prophets' intensity, so they responded by screaming out to their god, even gashing their bodies with swords and lances until the blood literally gushed out of them. They were convinced Baal would see how serious and dedicated they were to him and have pity and send fire. But Baal didn't send so much as a spark. Not even a warm breeze! He spoke not a word. Not even a syllable. Scripture records, "they raved until about 3:00 p.m.; but there was no voice, no one answered, and no one paid attention" (1 Kings 18:29).

"Give it a rest," Elijah tells the prophets. Then he invites all the people of Israel to come near. "Watch this," he says. Then he rebuilt the dismantled altar of the Lord with twelve stones, after which he dug a trench around it. After this, he instructed the people to drench the altar and fill the trench with water…lots and lots of water, 12 pitchers to be exact. "What's the big deal about that?" you ask. Not much, really, until you remember that Israel was suffering through a three-and-a-half year drought. Three-and-a-half years with no rain. There was no running water, no faucets, no drink machines, no snow cones, no iced cappuccinos and no bottled water. So you can imagine why water must have been a pretty scarce commodity. Yet in spite of this, Elijah dumps all this water on the altar, thoroughly soaking the wood. They must have thought him crazy, but it was all a part of Elijah's master plan. If God really did answer with fire, Elijah wanted no one to attribute it to dry wood, a spark, spontaneous combustion, or Baal showing up late. He didn't want anyone to accuse him of using trickery, illusion or slight of hand. If that wood, thoroughly marinated in water, caught fire, there could be only one explanation.

God.

The stage is now set. Tension fills the air as the crowd expectantly waits to see what will happen next. The prophets of Baal wipe the sweat from their brows while tending to their bloody cuts. Still panting from their frantic activity, their mouths are as parched as the Mount Carmel terrain. Elijah now begins calling out to the Lord.

> At the time of the offering of the *evening* sacrifice, Elijah the prophet came near and said, "O Lord, the God of Abraham, Isaac and Israel, today let it be known that You are God in Israel and that I am Your servant and I have done all these things at Your word. Answer me, O Lord, answer me, that this people may know that You, O Lord, are God, and *that* You have turned their heart back again. Then the fire of the LORD fell, and consumed the burnt offering and the wood and the stones and the dust, and licked up the water that was in the trench. (1 Kings 18:36–39)

Don't you love the imagery of the fire of God "licking up" the offering and the water? There was to be no mistaking exactly Who was answering Elijah's prayer. This phenomenon would not be explained away by some atmospheric anomaly or rogue lightning bolt. There wasn't a rain cloud in the sky. Hadn't been for three-and-a-half years. No one could claim Elijah had a box of matches hidden under his tunic. This was no ordinary fire. It was the "fire of the Lord," and it incinerated the ox, the wood, the stones, and the dust—even consuming the water! What a heat blast those people must have felt! Imagine the temperature on that mountain soaring several hundred degrees in a millisecond's time. This fire clearly originated from the sky for all to see, striking precisely on the altar the man of God had built.[73]

Yes, it was a *God Thing*.

Unmistakably. Unequivocally. Undeniably.

And every eyewitness to the event was fully persuaded. And as if choreographed, all the people fell on their faces and began repeating, "The LORD, He is God; the LORD, He is God." (1 Kings 18:39)

So humbled was the congregation, they couldn't even *look* towards the altar. Instead, they pressed their singed beards and faces into the still warm ground. The only thing cold there that day was the chill running down each spine. And nobody was "high-fiving" Elijah. This wasn't about him. The people weren't flat on their faces in fearful praise to the prophet. Whatever clout or presence Elijah enjoyed as spokesman for God was instantly overshadowed by the spectacular display of God's power. By showing up there that day, Yahweh proved He was the only true God and that Baal was an impotent, false deity. Ahab's pagan god was not real. And, therefore, the idea of him was certainly not worth worshiping. The God of Israel had filled Mount Carmel with His presence, hands down demonstrating He alone is worthy of our worship. It was a God-moment meant to restore His people's hearts back to Himself. And it worked.

Okay, now, be honest. Haven't you ever secretly wished God would do something just like that today? Just to do something proving to unbelievers, atheists and skeptics that He is the true God? Just to show those who pray in vain to Allah, Krishna, Buddha, or some other fictitious god that no one is listening. They cry out to the god of Islam, but he must be busy. They chant to the gods of Eastern Mysticism, but they are silent.

According to Jesus, a day is coming when all the nations will know He is God and God alone. Once He rescues His church from His coming wrath in the Tribulation, there will be no doubt as to Who occupies Heaven's throne.[74] And then, at His Second Coming, every eye will see Him.[75] And we will worship Him forever as He reigns supremely for eternity. That's what you're asking for every time you pray, "Your kingdom come, Your will be done on earth as it is in Heaven." You're asking God to come down and show up once and for all. And that's exactly what He has promised to do.

> According to Jesus, a day is coming when all the nations will know He is God and God alone.

In the meantime, we may sometimes experience a "righteous restlessness" whenever it seems evil is winning over good. And that makes us long for a spiritual showdown for all to see. In reality,

There's a little "Elijah" in all of us. A bit of sarcasm. A touch of boldness. A passion for justice. A desire for God to show the nations how real our God is.

We live in an age when God still does great miracles. He still punches a hole through our reality, injecting a supernatural happening into our earthly experience. But these God-Moments are limited to fire falling from Heaven or water turning into wine. And we fall prey to fleshly deception when we seek a repetition of biblical miracles. As Jesus Himself said, "An evil and adulterous generation seeks a sign."[76] And why did He say this? Because the Jews of His day were so preoccupied with seeing a miracle, they became blind to the miracle God was doing right in front of them! Prophecy was being fulfilled through the Person who was speaking to them, and they missed it. Instead, Christ pointed them back to the Scriptures.

Energized by His Spirit, faith in God's Word is what births those God-Moments in and through us. And while He does choose to wow us with the occasional over-the-top miracle—healings, divine protection, and prayer-fueled checks in the mail—our motivation for worship remains grounded in the truth of His Word. It's there where we clearly see who this God really is, what He has done, and done for *us*. And it is through our immersion into the Word that our minds and hearts are soaked in His vintage truth. *That* is what enables us to recognize the fingerprint of Almighty God on our lives, service and circumstances.

Albert Einstein once said, "There are two ways to live your life. One is as though nothing is a miracle. The other is as though everything is a miracle."

You don't need fire to fall from the sky in order to worship God. You just need to see and acknowledge those sometime subtle, supernatural snapshots that reveal His presence and power in your everyday life. Look for them. Be ready for them. And worship because it truly was a "God-Thing."

CHAPTER 10

# When Your World is Falling Apart

You would have seen more than your share of divine experiences had you been one of the original twelve disciples. Hanging out with Jesus every day for some three-and-a-half years, you would have accumulated a ton of amazing stories to one day share with family and friends. Many, though certainly not all, of those stories are faithfully recorded for us in the Gospel accounts. Had you kept a journal, you couldn't possibly document all those God-Moments. That's because Jesus Christ was a miracle-working Messiah. And because He was also 100% Man, Christ also did many other, more ordinary things with His disciple-friends. He ate with them, walked with them, traveled together with them and engaged in everyday, normal conversations. In His incarnation and identification with humanity, in many ways, He was no different than they were. Nevertheless, they were the Twelve Disciples, and as part of Jesus' inner circle, they were privileged to hear private messages and see miracles the crowds never witnessed. One of those miraculous moments is recorded in chapter four of Mark's gospel. It took place one night on the Sea of Galilee.

Jesus had led His disciples into a boat, and they began sailing to the other side of the sea. As they were making their way across, as they had done numerous times before, a "fierce gale of wind" arose suddenly. Such violent storms are not uncommon on the Sea of Galilee, occurring still today. At 670 feet below sea level, winds rush down from the surrounding 9,000-foot mountains, creating sudden storms, which cause dangerous and life-threatening conditions for vessels on the water. In this incident, the disciples' boat was being tossed around like a paper cup on the ocean. Soon, waves began crashing over the sides of the small vessel, so much so that it began filling up with water. Realizing they were in imminent danger, they instinctively began bailing as fast as they could. However, Mark tells us that in the midst of all this panic and peril, Jesus remained sound asleep in the back of the boat. But why would He be asleep? And how *could* He be? How does anyone sleep through a tempestuous storm like this? Was Jesus narcoleptic? Did He hit His head and black out? Was He only pretending to be asleep?

> Jesus Christ was a miracle-working Messiah. And because He was also 100% Man, Christ also did many other, more ordinary things with His disciple-friends. He ate with them, walked with them, traveled together with them and engaged in everyday, normal conversations.

Negative. A simple explanation clarifies why Jesus was unaffected and undisturbed by the wind, water and storm.

He was tired.

This wasn't a power nap. Jesus was experiencing what we in the South call being "bone tired"—some areas call it "dog tired." It's a weariness that goes past heavy eyelids, achy muscles, and sore feet. It's the kind that physically depletes your physical resources. There is not a part of you that isn't exhausted. That's where Jesus was. Worn out. Beat. Bushed. Done in. Dead on His feet. Drained. Down for the count. Fatigue had filled every cell in His body to the point that He could no longer remain conscious. And why? Consider what kind of day Jesus had been through. He began beside the Sea of Galilee. The crowd following Him swelled so large that He was forced to climb into a boat to keep from being overcome by them. This was the same "great multitude" from a day or so earlier.

> But Jesus withdrew with His disciples to the sea. And a great multitude from Galilee followed Him; and from Judea, and Jerusalem, and Idumea and beyond the Jordan; and these from Tyre and Sidon, a great multitude, when they heard how many things He was doing, came to Him. So He told His disciples that a small boat should be kept ready for Him because of the multitude, lest that they should crush Him; (Mark 3:7–9 ESV)

Picture this massive crowd pressing in on Jesus. It became a potentially dangerous situation because this crowd wasn't spiritually motivated. In a heartbeat, they could easily turn from a mild-manner multitude into a malicious mob. In fact, at least one other time in His ministry, the crowds intended to take Him by force and make Him King.[77] He knew how volatile the political climate was, and without much provocation, a riot or revolt could quickly form. So Jesus was careful to put Himself at a safe distance during such times. He also knew that by standing in a boat on the water with the people on the shore, the acoustics would be much more conducive to hearing His messages.

But more to the reason for His exhaustion. Jesus had spent every waking hour that day teaching "many things," including parables and principles concerning spiritual living, all the while standing or sitting in the that same boat.[78] As any preacher, teacher, or public speaker will tell you, speaking to a crowd of people will drain your physical and emotional energy. And Jesus did it all day long.

I once did a speaking tour of schools in a very poor region of Kentucky. These kids had never met a real author, so my hosts were eager to get me in front of as many students as possible. I ended up speaking to nine different school assemblies in two days, plus church services in the evenings and the following Sunday. I don't remember what I got paid, but I do, however, remember arriving home, physically wrecked and hardly able to string two coherent sentences together!

Jesus did way more than I. And as a result, His body was shot. His energy gone. His physical and emotional tank bone dry. And as a man, He desperately needed rest.

Can you identify with that? Ever worked so hard you didn't think you would make it till bedtime because you were so tired? Ever fall asleep in your clothes? On top of the covers? Ever woken up in the bathtub, the previously hot water now cool and still, wondering what time it was? Did you pull an all-nighter to study for an exam and afterwards felt like sleeping until the next millennium? Ever fall asleep sitting up? Or almost doze off at the wheel because your eyelids felt like they had lead weights attached to them? Ever had your eyes cross on you? Most of us have experienced times like these when you felt as if you would fall asleep standing up.

*That's* where Jesus was.

Now with their boat in the storm, the disciples scrambled to stay topside. And looking at Jesus, they couldn't figure out how or why the Lord could still be asleep during such a violent storm. Of course, being the levelheaded, spiritual, and courageous men that they were, they did what any group of future apostles would do in a situation like this.

They panicked.

"...they awoke Him and said to Him, 'Teacher, do You not care that we are perishing?'" (Mark 4:38)

Now keep playing this scene in your mind. It's pitch dark on the Sea of Galilee. The wind is howling. The storm is raging. Waves are crashing over the side of the small boat as it rocks back and forth. The rain is falling in horizontal sheets. Propelled by the fierce wind, it pelts them like needles. Grown men and professional fishermen are holding on for dear life, white-knuckling the sides of the boat, hugging the mast and one another like a two-year-old clinging to his mother's leg. Anything to keep them from being thrown overboard. They can hardly see through the watery curtain, and they're soaked from head to toe. And in the chaos of the moment, one of them must have shouted, "Somebody wake the Master!" And the other eleven responded scrambling to the back of the boat. Considering the noise created by the storm, they potentially had to crawl or climb over one another in order to wake Jesus. If so, this would not have been the smartest move, considering the current situation and the resulting weight redistribution in the small craft. But when you're in a crisis, little else matters as getting help becomes priority.

Eventually, they manage to shake Jesus out of His deep slumber. And upon doing so, the first thing they do is to accuse Him of not caring about them.

"We're dying over here, Lord! And You're sleeping on the job. We thought You cared. Why are You allowing this storm? Where were You when we needed You? We gave up everything to follow You and look what happened? Save us, Lord!"

Don't you find it interesting that as soon as the storm hit, their first thought was that God didn't care about them? In their distress, they equated problems and difficult circumstances with God not caring. Sound familiar? Ever wondered where God was in your storm? Have you ever felt like He was asleep, oblivious, or apathetic to your suffering? Maybe you called on Him, but all you got was more wind and rain. In the midst of your crisis, it appeared as if God had given up on you. You felt alone. Forgotten. The tempest swirling in your life seemed as if it would last forever. Your dark night may have even been accompanied by despair and even prolonged depression. You wondered why God would allow this to happen to you. And as the wind and rain pelted your soul, you shook your head in disbelief, crying out. "God, don't You care that I am perishing?"

That's where the disciples were that night. If Peter could step out of that boat and off the pages of Scripture, he just might put a drenched hand on your shoulder, look you straight in the eyes and confess, "We all know how you feel."

But what Peter and his fellow frightened friends didn't yet realize was that this storm was actually a "pop quiz" in disguise, given by Jesus to test their faith. The raging sea and black night were merely a backdrop against which God was about to display His glory. Like a master artist, God was on the verge of brush-stroking a miracle into their life portrait.

> Ever wondered where God was in your storm? Have you ever felt like He was asleep, oblivious, or apathetic to your suffering?

At this point, Jesus wakes up and immediately issues two strong rebukes: One to the wind and waves, and the other to the disciples.

And being aroused, He rebuked the wind and said to the sea, "Hush, be still." And the wind died down and it became perfectly calm. (Mark 4:39)

The translated phrase "be still" is the same Greek word Jesus used when He told the demon in Mark 1:25 to "be quiet!"—literally, *Shut up!* Here, Jesus is effectively commanding the gale force wind and the huge waves to immediately cease activity. But merely stopping the wind alone wouldn't have caused the sudden calm, for the waves would have continued to rock the boat. That's why Jesus' words went out to both the wind *and* the waves. And they did exactly what He commanded them to do. In an instant, the weather pattern changed. Had you been a meteorologist tracking radar that evening, a storm pattern would have instantly disappeared from your screen. Jesus commanded the water molecules to stop moving since nature's elements fell under His control. He had created both the Sea of Galilee and the mountains surrounding it. He knew the composition and history of every drop of water in that sea. And like every other force in the universe, they were subject to His will.[79] As God in human flesh, Jesus was able to do things only God could do—forgive sins (Matthew 9:6), impart divine truth (Mark 1:27), exercise authority over unclean spirits (Luke 4:36), execute judgment (John 5:27), and possess all authority in Heaven and earth (Matthew 28:18), including authority over creation itself. The Son of God suspended the laws of nature for His own purposes, as He did at other times when restoring health, regenerating eyesight, raising the dead, and rearranging the composition of H2O by changing it into fine wine. We call those things "miracles." And it happened in the split second He rebuked that storm.

His second rebuke, however, was reserved for His disciples.

And He said to them, "Why are you so timid? How is it that you have no faith?" (Mark 4:40)

Upon first glance, Jesus' reaction sounds a bit harsh, doesn't it? After all, his friends were scared out of their sandals, right? They just needed Him to "be there" for them. Isn't that why He's there? Didn't the Lord understand that?

So was He being too tough on them? Or was He just grumpy from having been abruptly woken from His nap?

> Jesus is our friend and we take great comfort from knowing He identifies with us in our humanity.

To begin, the disciples were very afraid, a natural reaction when you're facing a potentially life-threatening situation like theirs. It would be the equivalent of being on a flight and hearing a sudden explosion. The plane begins rapidly descending, losing altitude and cabin pressure. Oxygen masks deploy. The huge jet is now diving towards the earth at 600mph as you look up to see a hole the size of a Honda Civic in the fuselage. Are you ready to panic, yet? Can you feel the fear?" It's a safe bet no one is breathing normally.

That's where the disciples are—only without the oxygen masks. So we can see why they initially freaked. But consider for a minute just Who it was in that boat with them. It wasn't the captain of the sailing club, or some Galilean lifeguard. It was God Almighty. The Creator and King of the Universe was in that fishing boat. So the obvious question then becomes, "Should the disciples have known this already?"

Answer: Yes.

But why? Why should they have had the kind of faith that would have kept them being filled with fear? Several reasons: First, they had been eyewitnesses to Jesus' other miracles, clearly proving to them that He was more than just a teacher. Of course, they may have rationalized and reasoned of His previous miracles, "Sure, He may be able to heal a leper, but this is a full-fledged storm here!" Like you and me, they may have suffered from short-term memory loss. We tend to forget the things God does for us, right? Either way, their fear overrode their confidence in Him.

Second, they had heard Jesus say, "Let *us* go to the other side"(Mark 4:35). He didn't say, "Hey guys, let's all take a voyage to the bottom of the sea." Instead, He had already promised them safe arrival. They should have, therefore, taken Him at His word. Third, Jesus Himself was with them in their boat. Did they really think He was going to drown?

But enough about the disciples. What about you? How would you have responded to Jesus in the same situation? Had you been in the boat that night and experienced this moment, would you have exhibited a similar level of panic? Upon witnessing His power over nature, would you have shouted, "Wow, Jesus! That was so cool! How'd You do that?" Would you have given Him a "thumbs up" from the back of the boat? Not likely. Sure, Jesus is our friend and we take great comfort from knowing He identifies with us in our humanity. But seeing and experiencing this kind of event up close produces a radically different response in us. Had you been there, you would no longer be thinking about wind or waves. It wouldn't matter that you were soaked in seawater from head to toe. The reality of what just took place would have shaken you, even as it did the Twelve.

Now a different kind of wave came crashing into that boat. A wave of fear. A surge of awe. A reverential swell washing over each of them. Their fear was actually much greater now than it had ever been while in the storm. Looking around "…they became very much afraid and said to one another, 'Who then is this, that even the wind and the sea obey Him?'" (Mark 4:41)

Dr. Luke tells us they were "fearful and amazed."[80] Perhaps for the very first time, they realized they were in the presence of Deity. God was in their boat. Or rather, they were in *His*.

The sea was now calm. Hardly a breeze was blowing in the cool night air. The humidity level had dropped dramatically. Can you see one of the Twelve carefully picking up an oar and slowly beginning to row. Odds are, no one is speaking because they had all been rendered mute by Jesus' marvelous miracle. They are astonished. Bewildered. Fear and amazement has gripped them. Had it not happened to them all, each man may have wondered if it was all a dream. But what occurred that stormy night was undeniably very real. As they neared the other side of the sea, most of the disciples were likely contemplating the supernatural phenomenon they had just experienced. Others perhaps were gazing at Jesus. He, of course, knew something they didn't—yet another miracle was about to occur once they set foot on solid ground.[81] Things are moving fast as they are still processing this most recent miracle. What should they do with this new revelation Jesus has given them concerning Himself?

Surely from this point on, the disciples would look at Christ through a brand new set of eyes. They would interpret subsequent events and experiences through a whole new theological grid. Their perspective had changed. They had changed. *Everything* had changed because God allowed the blinding light of His deity to come bursting through space and time, landing right there in a Galilean fishing boat.

Aren't you ever jealous that the disciples saw and experienced so many of these supernatural events? Or maybe you wonder why they were so slow to "get it?" Why Jesus had to teach them truths time and again before they finally understood them? I mean, what was wrong with these guys?

Keep in mind, the original disciples didn't have Internet, Bible apps or even Bibles! There were no leather-bound translations of Scripture, complete with study notes, maps, concordances, cross references, summaries and outlines of each book. Instead, it all went down "live" for them. Everything happened in the moment. The New Testament was being fleshed out right before their eyes, years before any of them would ever pick up a quill to faithfully record what they had seen and heard. There was no "church," though they themselves would soon see it birthed.

But to their credit, the disciples didn't always flunk the test. They may have been slow, but they sure were determined in their faith. Eventually—particularly following the resurrection, ascension, and coming of the Holy Spirit—they all "got it." They unashamedly declared Christ and His gospel to their world, suffering horribly for it. Some were crucified, while others were beaten, banished, boiled in oil, butchered and beheaded. And you can bank on this: Every one of those disciples used their last breath to worship the One who commands the wind and the waves.

## So What's the "Benefit Package?"

Sometimes, God shows up in ways that are undeniable, unavoidable and unmistakable. His presence and power are put on display before us in such a manner that trying to explain it in any other way would just be plain dumb. You would have to be blind not to see it. There is a measurable, concrete, tangible result since the overwhelming evidence points to Him. He simply worked on your behalf, changing circumstances and you. And once again, those God-moments can arrive without spiritual fireworks, coming more subtly, gradually, almost in a whisper. Often they occur when a Scripture seems to leap off the page of your Bible and right into your heart and mind. Though you may have read the same passage hundreds of times, you are somehow able to see it in a way you never have before. Or it happens in a worship service when a pastor or teacher explains a passage in a way that opens your understanding in a fresh, life-changing way. That's the Holy Spirit creating a very special worship for you.

> Sometimes, God shows up in ways that are undeniable, unavoidable and unmistakable. His presence and power are put on display before us.

But no matter how they come, they are always glorious because of what they do for our worship. And we should never walk away from them unchanged, especially when our world seems to be crumbling all around us. David had a unique perspective on times like these.[82]

And yet, even when the pain shouts despair and defeat in your ears, you must tune your spirit to hear God. And why? Because of what He wishes to accomplish in and through you.

First, these experiences reveal something about God. They tell you He is there. That He is real and powerful. That He is listening and that He still cares. That He is still invading your time and space. They give you hope in knowing that God is alive in your world. Face it. The Lord doesn't always rescue you from the storm. Sometimes, He simply rides it out with you. It's just another way of saying He's there, and that He will never leave your side, no matter how bad life gets.[83] It's been said, "Sometimes He calms the storm while, at other times, He calms His child?"

Second, these experiences uncover a lot about you and your level of faith. Like an x-ray machine, these experiences uncover things about us not easily seen from the outside. When God does something unusual, that encounter can expose shallowness, weakness, impatience, fear, immaturity and hidden pride living within us. It can purge us. But that cleansing also releases a joy within us. As we see our weaknesses brought to the surface, it only causes us to realize how much more we desperately need Him. It should motivate us to keep growing in intimacy with Him each day.

Third, your worship often kicks in while still within your "life-storm." It is in the crucible of pain that God often delights to visit you. In fact, the greatest yet most powerful unexplainable experiences with God come through your pain. It's then you are most vulnerable and dependent. As John Hercus has said, we must "trust God even when the pieces don't fit." And in difficult times, the pieces rarely seem to fit. In the blinding rain of real life, when you are often at your weakest point, His strength becomes your greatest sufficiency (2 Corinthians 12:9). It is during those times when you gain a sustaining strength and peace. That supernatural supply holds you up and sometimes holds you *together*. God pours out

His grace, often in a moment's time...just for you. Don't fear the storm, fellow believer. Know that He is right there with you in your boat.

Fourth, meeting God in the storm erases preconceived ideas you may have had about Him. Though you and I can know God personally, we can never completely figure out all His ways. At times He simply demonstrates for us that He is God. Those times may occur when our faith and prayer expectation level is peaking. When we're risking much for His kingdom, giving, trusting, persevering—that's when He shows up for us. These moments prevent us from stuffing the Almighty into a neat little "box" in our minds. They tell us we will never figure out all the ways He works. And He *really does* work in mysterious ways. His will and His ways are *still* not ours.[84]

The disciples were forced to do this in their boat experience. They thought Jesus would rescue them from the storm. The storm didn't quite fit their theology and their image of God and His ways. They were forced to jettison their preconceived ideas about Him, and so should we. We must allow His Word to mold our thinking regarding who He is. And when He allows things to happen which are contrary to how we think He should act, we have to surrender our wills to His. These experiences teach us that while His ways cannot always be traced, His heart can always be trusted.

Finally, the point of worshiping when your world is falling apart is ultimately to exalt God. As we respond to these awesome displays of God in and around our lives, we will be moved to worship in various ways. Sometimes, the best thing to do is just be silent and still—like the disciples probably did after Jesus calmed the storm. Other times, we will be impressed with a need to submit our lives in a fresh or deeper way to Him—like the people of God at Mount Carmel. Or we may be inspired to rise up and do something great for God in strength—like the army of Israel after God made the Sun stand still. We may even desire to memorialize the experience—like the stone memorial Joshua built after God showed up at the defeat of Jericho.

You may also choose to make or establish something in His honor to remember in the months and years to come. But the best thing about praising Him in the storm is that He gets all the credit. The glory and honor is all due Him. As Paul wrote in Romans 11:36, For from Him and through Him and to Him are all things. To Him be the glory forever. Amen.

No matter how small your boat or how big your storm, He is still there. He's not panicking and He wont let you drown. Worship Him while you rock back and forth. Worship Him while the wind and rain push and pelt against you. And worship Him when He chooses to tell the storm to "Shut up!"

It's then you'll experience first-hand the answer to the disciples' question, "Who then is this, that even the wind and the sea obey Him?"

CHAPTER 11

# Royal Want Ads
## God is Seeking Worshipers

> But an hour is coming, and now is, when the true worshipers shall worship the Father in spirit and truth; for such people the Father seeks to be His worshipers.
> – John 4:23

## The "Seeker-Sensitive" God?

As Christians, we are accustomed to sermons and messages urging us to "seek God." Ironically, some churches have even been described as "seeker-sensitive" as if unbelievers could somehow seek after Him. God's Word clearly denies this possibility. In fact, the opposite is true, as men and women continually run from their Creator, seeking self and sin instead.[85] What is often omitted or ignored is that God Himself is the real Seeker. According to Scripture, He is the One who is looking for *us*! Generally speaking, He seeks sinners, the lost, those dead in sin.[86]

But what else does God long for? What does His heart desire? What kind of person is He seeking today? What does He consider His "treasure"—that for which He is willing to search the whole earth? As you journey through Scripture, you eventually come upon passages that reveal that for which God is searching.

For example, in Ezekiel 22:30, the Lord is searching for someone who will "stand in the gap before Me for the land, that I should not destroy it," though at that time, He found no one. The prophet Jeremiah was instructed by God to "Roam to and fro through the streets of Jerusalem, And look now, and take note. And seek in her open squares, If you can find a man, If there is one who does justice, who seeks truth, Then I will pardon her."⁸⁷ Again, not a single person was found. Then there's the prophet Hanani, who revealed a principle to King Asa of Judah regarding another type of person sought by God. "For the eyes of the LORD move to and fro throughout the earth that He may strongly support those whose heart is completely His" (2 Chronicles 16:9).

However, Jesus uncovers yet one more category of believers for which the heart of God longs to find. This search supersedes all previous ones. This is the *big one*. A treasure like no other. More valuable than silver. More precious than gold. It's something more dear to His heart than planets, kingdoms, and angels. It's something so cherished by Him that he will one day populate all of Heaven with these rare people. So what He is seeking? What is so priceless to Yahweh? Here it is: What gladdens His heart is a special kind of people.

Worshipers.

More specifically, He has a certain type of worshiper in mind. This kind of worshiper does more than sing loudly or lift his or her hands during the music portion of church service. This kind of Christian understands worship as something more than a Sunday activity. It's even more than worship as a *lifestyle*. This person sees worship as an integral part of his or her *identity*. I *am* a worshiper of God. It's my ultimate place and purpose in life and eternity. This is the kind of worshiper that touches the heart of God with spiritual intimacy.

> I am a worshiper of God. It's my ultimate place and purpose in life and eternity.

## Wonderful Stranger

About 6 months into His public ministry, Jesus decides to head north from Judea into Galilee. To get there, He and the disciples could have chosen from three possible routes, the first was west along the Mediterranean Sea while the other lay east and followed the Jordan River. Both of these would have meant long journeys. Instead, Jesus chose a third travel option, which meant traveling a straight path north to Galilee—a route leading them right through the heart of Samaria. After all, the shortest distance between two points is a straight line, right? True. And due to the fact that Jesus was never One to needlessly waste time, this choice made perfect sense. He was well aware that His stay on earth was limited and rapidly approaching an end. So it would have seemed a prudent thing for Him to lead His disciples this way. However, there was one slight problem. Traveling this route would take them right through what the Jews considered "no man's land." The region of Samaria was deemed *off limits* to Jews because Samaritans were considered inferior. In fact, they detested Samaritans with a deep-rooted animosity that dated back hundreds of years. Here's why:

> The Samaritan people were a mixed race: half Jew and half Gentile. Their roots trace back about 700 years before Christ when the Assyrians held Israel captive. During that captivity, Jewish men took Assyrian women as their wives and, well…there you have it. But in addition to being a racially mixed people, they also were a *religious* mix as well. Because of their half-Jewish heritage, they combined Jewish and pagan religions to form a sort of hybrid faith. Though it contained some basic elements of God's truth, it wasn't an orthodox faith in the true God. The Samaritans even had their own temple and special "holy place" to worship. For these reasons and many others, Jews avoided Samaritans. And they came up with ways to demonstrate their disdain. When a Jew wanted to insult or degrade someone, he called him a "Samaritan"—if you recall, Jesus was labeled a demon-possessed Samaritan in John 8:48. This hatred was so bad that some Pharisees prayed that no Samaritan would be raised in the resurrection![88] And though done for other reasons, Jesus Himself initially forbade His disciples to take the Gospel to Samaria, but only to go to the "lost sheep of Israel."[89] But upon the Holy Spirit's entrance into the world at Pentecost, Christ commanded His followers to proclaim the Good News in "Judea, Samaria, and the uttermost parts of the earth" (Acts 1:8).

So Jesus leads His disciples to the other side of the tracks to visit this forbidden region of Samaria. They hike roughly 25–30 miles until they reach a city called

> "Sychar, near the parcel of ground that Jacob gave to his son Joseph; and Jacob's well was there. Jesus therefore, being wearied from His journey, was sitting thus by the well. It was about the sixth hour." John 4:5

So pause and think about this for a minute. Jesus has just walked the equivalent of a marathon. Not in a pair of $120 running shoes, but rather in first-century, leather-laced sandals. No moisture-absorbing running socks back then. It was a very long walk. Arriving around 6pm in Sychar, Jesus is understandably exhausted from the journey, and so He rests by a well while His disciples go into town in search of food. But while He is sitting there, a woman carrying a water pot walks up. Because His lips were no doubt parched and His throat dry, and because He had no way of drawing water out of the well, Jesus requests a drink to quench His thirst.

Startled, the woman replied, "How is it that You, being a Jew, ask me for a drink since I am a Samaritan woman?" (John 4:9)

Now here was one savvy woman. From her question, we can discern that she recognized Jesus as a Jew, probably from His dress and dialect. We don't normally think of Jesus having a particular accent, but He did. He likely spoke like every other Jewish man from Galilee. But beyond His accent, this woman was also well aware of the difference and divide between Jews and Samaritans. She knew what Jewish men thought of her race. She was also aware it was "taboo" for a Hebrew man to speak in public with a Samaritan woman. Unfortunately, women were second-class citizens in those days, forbidden to vote or hold public office. However, Jesus and Christianity would soon begin changing all that. Not only did women become the chief financial supporters of Christ's ministry (Luke 8:3), they were also among His most devoted followers (Luke 10:35–42). Women were the ones honored to be the first witnesses of the resurrected Christ at the tomb and privileged to be the first to tell the world He was alive (Mark 16:9–10). For these and many other reasons, the female gender found a welcome and true friend in Jesus Christ.

But this particular woman wasn't yet thinking of Jesus in this way. She was too amazed that He had spoken to her in the first place. Perhaps she was also wondering what this man's real motives were in striking up a conversation with her.

## #awkward

Suddenly, Jesus changes the subject. Laying aside His own physical thirst, He instead concentrates on the woman's *spiritual* need. Throwing her a verbal curveball, He turns the topic towards God. As you probably already know, that can create a world of tension in the midst of a casual conversation. This wasn't the time for Jesus to "earn the right to be heard" or to build a friendship *with* her. He didn't have the luxury of allowing her to observe His life and become convinced of who He was. He simply saw an opportunity and dove right in.

But He also saw into this woman's heart like no mortal could. And what He observed was a lifetime of sin, hurt, disappointment, and shame. Peering into her soul, He saw an unfulfilled woman locked in a desperate search for love and satisfaction. She was caught in a self-perpetuated, depressing cycle of unfulfilled relationships, looking for love in all the wrong places and faces. And so, knowing her situation, Jesus goes right for the jugular.

> Startled, the woman replied, "How is it that You, being a Jew, ask me for a drink since I am a Samaritan woman?" (John 4:9)

> Jesus answered and said to her, "If you knew the gift of God, and who it is who says to you, 'Give Me a drink,' you would have asked Him, and He would have given you living water."
>
> She *said to Him, "Sir, You have nothing to draw with and the well is deep; where then do You get that living water?
>
> "You are not greater than our father Jacob, are You, who gave us the well, and drank of it himself, and his sons, and his cattle?"
>
> Jesus answered and said to her, "Everyone who drinks of this water shall thirst again; but whoever drinks of the water that I shall give him shall never thirst; but the water that I shall give him shall become in him a well of water springing up to eternal life." (John 4:10–14)

Were it not so true, it would almost be funny. Here is a man, covered in dust, his robe and undergarments sweaty-damp from a full day's walk in the sun, and not smelling too good. The arid mountain desert has scorched His lips. His body is fatigued and His throat dry. His parched throat is desperate for a cool drink . . . and yet He's offering *her* water! What a paradox. Our Lord lays aside the familiar gratification of that first sip of cool well water for something infinitely more important to Him. Using divine discernment, Jesus has just diagnosed the exact source of her problem. Like a sunken wreckage, in the depths of her heart lay the scattered debris and remains of a life without hope. And so, instead of lowering a water pot down into the well, He drops a truth anchor instead. Jesus turns the conversation and her world upside down by offering her spiritual water that forever satisfies the thirst of the human soul. Suddenly, it's *her* lips that seem parched. Her throat is dry. Her soul is weary and thirsting for something more. This water of which Jesus speaks sounds like what she has been looking for all these years.

She bears some resemblance to Nicodemus in John's previous chapter as she too fails to connect the spiritual meaning of His words. And as with Nicodemus, Christ gets more specific with her.

> Salvation did come first to the Jews as God's covenant people. The very first Christians were Jewish believers.

Strangely, He tells her to "go get your husband." But why would He say something like this? Was He tired of talking to her? Did He suddenly realize He was breaking social etiquette by speaking with her? Was He being rude, sexist, or racist? Of course not. Far from being an unkind comment, Jesus knows that before she can receive the pure water He offers, she must first recognize something about *herself*. Look what happens next:

> The woman answered and said, "I have no husband." Jesus said to her, "You have well said, 'I have no husband'; for you have had five husbands, and the one whom you now have is not your husband; this you have said truly." (John 4:17–18)

This poor woman had been married five times and was currently living with a sixth man. There was no way she would ever experience true human love until she came to know the One who Himself is love.[90] She had jumped from one relationship to the next, having been passed around from man to man. And each one had failed to give her what she really longed for. Never had a man told her what she really needed to hear, or even cared to. Until now. That's because this particular Man was different. Very different. Jesus wasn't after a romantic or physical relationship with her. He wasn't just one more guy who wanted to take something from her. His motives were pure as the water from that nearby well.

Because of this supernatural declaration, she responded, "Sir, I perceive that You are a prophet."

Correct, for who else would know so much about her personal life?

So now, believing Him to be a prophet—and obviously a Jewish one—she engages Him in a conversation about race and religion. Specifically, the topic was "Who's right? The Jews or Samaritans regarding the proper place to worship God?" Jesus answers her stating that it's not *where* you worship that is of upmost importance. Rather it's *Who* you worship that really counts. He then adds, "You Samaritans have totally missed the truth regarding the worship of God. We worship the true God, for God has revealed Himself to the Jews. The Messiah will come from the Jews as well."[91]

He was right of course. Salvation did come first to the Jews as God's covenant people. The very first Christians were Jewish believers. Once again, Jesus is not being racist or arrogant, but instead He is being lovingly straightforward with her. He's not worried about offending this woman or invading her "safe space." He's not concerned about her thinking He is a bigot, racist or "Samariaphobe." And He wasn't about to bend God's truth or alter His plan of salvation just to avoid hurting her feelings. He knew that believing a lie about God—no matter how universally accepted it may be—is both heresy and idolatry (i.e. *not* worship). So He told her the truth, for her own spiritual good and eternal benefit.

The Son of God possessed the unique ability to declare unwavering truth to people while at the same time sincerely expressing love for the person. Of course, this same truth would later incite hatred from His own people and their leaders. But here, Jesus is informing her that now is the time to stop haggling over the primary physical location of worship.

"What's more important is that you actually *become* a true worshiper of God," He tells her. But what are the pre-requisites? The qualifications? Must this person be Jewish? Male? Religious? Educated? Wealthy? Not divorced? Having never sinned by "shacking up" with a partner?

Who exactly are these "true worshipers" of whom Jesus is describing?

## A True Worshiper's Heartbeat

Fortunately, He defines further for her (and us) what this kind of worshiper looks like. Jesus stipulates that whoever worships God must simply do so "in spirit and truth." It makes sense that since He is God, He alone determines the conditions for acceptable worship, right? So let's find out what each of these requirements for worship really means.

True worship involves the spirit because it is primarily a spiritual activity. This has to be so because God is Spirit. He doesn't dwell in a physical body or in a building made with human hands.[92] Though the Son of God took on human flesh and now dwells in a glorified body in Heaven, God in His nature is Spirit. He doesn't have "arms" or "eyes," though Scripture sometimes uses "anthropomorphic" (human) terms to help us comprehend certain characteristics about Him, such as His strength (arm) or His knowledge (eyes). That's why we have to worship Him in our spirit. Your spirit is the part of you that's "you." It's the part of you that experiences intimacy with God. To worship *in spirit* means our worship is primarily an inward experience. Though there can be outward physical expressions of worship, such as the ones we have seen in previous chapters, worship begins on the inside and is a matter of the spirit. This misplaced priority and focus was one of the biggest problems Jesus encountered with the Pharisees. Their worship was "skin-deep," and mostly external. But Jesus wanted His followers to focus on the heart, spirit, and inner person.

> "Beware of practicing your righteousness before men to be noticed by them; otherwise you have no reward with your Father who is in heaven". "And when you pray, you are not to be as the hypocrites; for they love to stand and pray in the synagogues and on the street corners, in order to be seen by men. Truly I say to you, they have their reward in full. "But you, when you pray, go into your inner room, and when you have shut your door, pray to your Father who is in secret, and your Father who sees in secret will repay you." (Matthew 6:1, 5–6)

For the Pharisees, worship was just another show. They wanted their worship to be seen by men. It was never about touching their spirits or connecting with their hearts, only about appearing religious and spiritual to others. For them, it was a performance. And in Christian culture today, that places a high value on *presentation* in church. This creates a blur between real worship and worship *activity*. Concert-driven church venues and stage personalities can easily, though unintentionally, divert attention away from the only One worthy of our honor and adulation.

"Not so for you," Jesus says. So whether you're alone or in a crowd of hundreds, worship must always be God-centered and a matter of the heart. True worship springs from the innermost part of you:

- It is in your spirit that you feel the deepest desires and emotions (John 11:33, 13:21).
- You serve God in your spirit (Romans 1:9).
- You cry out to God with your spirit (Romans 8:15).
- The Spirit bears witness with your spirit that you are His child (Romans 8:16).
- You pray in the Spirit (Jude 1:20).
- And you worship in the Spirit (Romans 12:1–2; Philippians 3:3).

> True worship involves the spirit because it is primarily a spiritual activity. This has to be so because God is Spirit. He doesn't dwell in a physical body or in a building.

God wants His children to worship in spirit, and that involves the whole heart—all of you. This was something the woman at the well had certainly never heard before. But there is another requirement God makes concerning our worship.

## The Integrity of Worship

Jesus' second requirement regarding worship is that it be done "in truth." There are at least three areas touched by Jesus' statement of worshiping "in truth." The first relates to hypocrisy. You may already be aware that the word *hypocrite* originally referred to Greek actors. An actor would wear a mask while playing a role on stage—one representing the mood of the character being portrayed. The actor himself really wasn't the character he played. He was just pretending, just like actors do today. "Don't wear a mask when you worship," Jesus is saying. "Don't pretend to worship when your heart isn't in it. Be the real you."

In other words, worshiping "in truth" means you are true to your sincere heart for God.

Once again, unfortunately, the Pharisees were role model hypocrites in this area. They spoke one way and lived another. They fulfilled Isaiah's prophecy of the people who honored God with their lips, but their hearts were far away from Him.[93] Jesus said their worship was empty and meaningless to God (Matthew 15:7–9). As leaders, the Pharisees became the "blind leading the blind." They prayed, but didn't really mean what they said. It was just an exercise in religiosity to them. Their worship was all about them. It was about appearance. They looked great on the outside but on the inside, Jesus said they stunk (Matthew 23:27).

Worshiping in truth means there will be times when your emotions are *flat-lining*. In fact, this will often be our experience because our emotions tend to ebb and flow—up and down and all over the map. You're worshiping, but you just aren't *feeling it*. That's okay. You can't look to your emotions to lead you in worship. If they come, fine. But they are the result of worship, not the cause of it. And don't ever fake it or try to work up an emotional feeling to motivate you.

I wonder, as Jesus walks among His churches all across our country, what He sees. As churchgoers sing, pray, serve, smile, give, and drink coffee, I wonder how much that shallow, external "spirit of the Pharisees" still haunts us? Our Lord warned us, "Therefore do not be like them" (Matthew 6:8). Those first-century religious leaders should have known better, considering they were regarded as Bible experts. But did they know the following verses?

"Now, therefore, fear the LORD and *serve Him in sincerity and truth*; and put away the gods which your fathers served beyond the River and in Egypt, and serve the LORD. (Joshua 14:14)

"Only fear the LORD and *serve Him in truth with all your heart*; for consider what great things He has done for you. (1 Samuel 12:24)

"Since I know, O my God, that Thou triest *the heart* and delightest in uprightness, I, in the *integrity of my heart*, have willingly offered all these things; so now with joy I have seen Thy people, who are present here, make their offerings willingly to Thee. (1 Chronicles 29:17)

(A Prayer of David.) Hear a just cause, O LORD, give heed to my cry; Give ear to my prayer, which is *not from deceitful lips*. (Psalm 17:1)

How blessed is the man to whom the LORD does not impute iniquity, And *in whose spirit there is no deceit*! (Psalm 32:2)

Behold, You *desire truth in the innermost being*, And in the hidden part You will make me know wisdom. (Psalm 51:6)

God desires a truthful heart from those who worship Him. That's why Jesus exposed this woman's sinful lifestyle. He wanted her to be a true worshiper, but before that could happen, she would first have to recognize her true condition before God. Her problem wasn't that she was a Samaritan or a woman. Her problem was that she was a sinner, and Jesus wanted her to acknowledge that in her heart.

But to worship "in truth" goes beyond admitting your sin. It also means having integrity concerning the truth about Jesus. Later in their conversation, Jesus would tell this woman He was the long-awaited Messiah. A pretty bold claim considering it made Him out to be equal with God! But this was a truth He asserted on many occasions (John 8:58–59, 10:29–33). So part of worshiping in truth means to worship God through Jesus Christ who *is* the Truth. Therefore, the only true worshipers are those who worship out of a right relationship to Him. The implications of this are obvious, not the least of which is that Christ is the only way to Heaven. As Messiah, He would naturally be the only way to the Father (John 14:6). He was the truth and full of God's truth (John 1:14). Paragraph. Period. End of discussion. Jesus Christ leaves no room for the worship of Buddha, Confucius, Mohammed, Allah or any other religion, faith or belief system. He made it clear that salvation is exclusively through Him. Again, if that sounds narrow-minded, it's because it is! But by its very nature and definition, truth is a very narrow-minded concept. Twelve inches will always equal one foot no matter who says it. Sixteen ounces is always one pound. A circle cannot be a square, or it ceases to be a circle. Yes, it is very narrow-minded to assert that two plus two is four and not five. But again, that's the nature of absolute truth. It's unbending and forever fixed. Jesus claimed to be "the truth" and there is simply no way to wiggle around that (John 14:6).

But there is a third implication of worshiping "in truth." It's that we must also be true to Scripture. Since the written revelation of God—the Bible—is everything we need for life and godliness, it stands to reason that our worship should conform to the truth of Scripture.[94] That means our worship of God is not based on what we "think" God is like or what we "feel" to be true about Him. We do not form thoughts about God or direct our worship of Him based on whims, feelings, or human impulse. True worship is grounded in knowledge, and that knowledge of God is according to the "word of truth." This means as we grow, our worship will have increasing substance and depth. Diving into Scripture over time enables us to think deep thoughts of God—thoughts worthy of Him—the Almighty, Infinite, Sovereign, Holy, Loving, Gracias, Righteous, Wrathful God of all there is.

No matter how long you have been a Christian or how much you have studied or think you know about God, there is still an eternity's worth left to discover about our awesome Lord. Remember Paul's words to the Philippians:

> "Not that I have already obtained it, or have already become perfect, but I press on in order that I may lay hold of that for which also I was laid hold of by Christ Jesus. Brethren, I do not regard myself as having laid hold of it yet; but one thing I do: forgetting what lies behind and reaching forward to what lies ahead, I

press on toward the goal for the prize of the upward call of God in Christ Jesus." (Philippians 3:12–14)

These verses give us a window into Paul's personal walk and intimacy with Christ. In them, He confesses he isn't satisfied with where he is, spiritually speaking. There was a healthy discontentment in his life. He knew he hadn't "arrived" yet. He still had miles to go before he could consider himself as having completed spiritual maturity. He hadn't yet achieved the level of Christ-likeness he desired. He wanted more. He wanted depth. Depth of knowledge. Depth of experience. Depth of insight. Depth of relationship. But what makes all this so incredible was that at the time he wrote this letter, Paul had known Jesus about 30 years! Yet even then, he still wanted to know Him more![95]

> He made it clear that salvation is exclusively through Him. Again, if that sounds narrow-minded, it's because it is! But by its very nature and definition, truth is a very narrow-minded concept.

What about you? Do you still desire more? Do you want to know more about Him? To know Him more intimately? Still want to go deeper, like you once did? To be honest, from the very start of this book, my intention was to take you a bit deeper than most. I didn't want to give you just another "Christian book." Instead, my vision was to challenge you to take your worship to the next level. A higher one. I don't want you to be satisfied with worshiping God at the infant or adolescent level. My prayer for you is that you praise Him with understanding, maturity, heart, and depth! My desire is that you worship in truth—with personal integrity, exclusive loyalty to Christ and with faithfulness to the Word of God.

## You with me?
### Worship that is Rare and Well-Done

Lastly, Jesus tells this Samaritan lady something about God she had not known before. He reveals to her the real purpose of His visit to the well at Sychar.

"But an hour is coming, and now is, when the true worshipers shall worship the Father in spirit and truth; for such people the Father seeks to be His worshipers." John 4:23

We've already discussed what it means to worship "in spirit and in truth," but two questions still remain: Are these kinds of worshipers common? Why does God long for these kinds of people? The answer to the first question is those who worship in spirit and truth are not as common as we might think. As you look around and observe your world, you will see there are common things and rare things, the ordinary and the extraordinary, the everyday normal and the exceptional. You can walk out in a field and unearth ordinary quartz crystals, but there's a much slimmer chance you will dig up diamonds. There's a difference between finding a penny in a parking lot and uncovering a gold coin off the Florida coast. Common things are abundant. Rare things are…well…*rare*!

Unfortunately, it's common for people to worship mindlessly, without really engaging. It's easy to worship because it's "that time" in the service. I've done that. We all have. It also goes without saying that most of us have engaged in outward expressions of worship without ever plugging in our hearts. That's pretty normal. But we do this because we miss and misunderstand worship itself. We also have a tendency at times to worship *worship*, to worship for the good feeling it brings, or even to praise God verbally out of habit or Christian social pressure. We worship when it's convenient, but scarcely engage in it when our lives are a mess. We complain, but we fail to simply worship God in the pain. But that's not being a "spirit and truth" worshiper, is it? Honest praise, even when in the midst of great difficulty, is still worship.

At times, you may even think you are one of the few true worshipers left. But you would be wrong. Do you remember how negative and depressed Elijah became after his great victory at Mount Carmel? After defeating the 450 prophets of Baal, he sat down under a tree and asked

God to take his life. Wow. Then he went into a cave and continued his personal pity party there, lamenting to God that he alone was left as a true servant of God. "It's just me, God. I am the only true worshiper you have." But the Lord was quick to inform His pitiful prophet that He had 7,000 in Israel who had not yet bowed to Baal (1 Kings 19:18). You see, that's how amazing and wonderful our God is. He has true worshipers all over your town, state, country and world. There are other worshipers in your school, church, profession, and community. He just wants to make sure you are one of them! A God as great as ours will always have true worshipers! Even in the Tribulation. That's how worthy He is. Meanwhile, every one of us is a work in progress. Every one a project God has promised never to abandon (Philippians 1:6). And that's great news.

Years ago, there was a popular Christian saying,

"Please be patient with me. God isn't finished with me yet."

You saw this everywhere from t-shirts to bumper stickers—the Internet of the day!

When Ruth Bell Graham, wife of famed evangelist Billy Graham, died in 2007, she had requested the following epitaph to be engraved on her tombstone:

> *"End of construction –*
> *thank you for your patience."*

And he isn't finished with you either. Our lives are so short, but what an honor it is to spend that time understanding what it means to bring joy to God's heart by worshiping Him well.

## Guess Who?

So did this Samaritan woman ever get it? Was her heart open to the things Jesus was saying to her? Following Jesus' revelation concerning true worshipers, she tells Him she is aware of the coming Messiah as "He will reveal all things to us" (John 4:25). Now here is a woman in desperate need of some good news. After all, what did she have to look forward to in her life? What was waiting for her at home but another day of despair? Though she had led a sinful lifestyle, there was still a small glimmer of hope in her heart that Messiah would come and fill in the blanks about God. Little did she know up until this point, but the great

Hope of the world was seated opposite her and was preparing to rock her world. Though His words so far had been surprising, informative and even convicting, Jesus was about to give her one more revelation.

The sun was likely setting above the Mediterranean as the sky gradually grew dark over Jacob's well. Even so, with each new sentence, Jesus progressively turned up the light for this Samaritan, revealing more and more of who He really was. He decides that now is the time for her to hear the whole truth about Him. She already knows He isn't an ordinary Jewish man. She is also convinced He isn't your average, run-of-the-mill orthodox Jewish prophet. He was way too kind for that. Too genuinely interested. Too caring. Too personal. Too spiritual.

He had led her heart and thoughts throughout the entire conversation, and now she was at a point to receive a truth she could not possibly have handled back when He first asked her for that drink of water. She may have had suspicions about Him before, but nothing in her mind could have prepared her for what He was about to say.

Jesus said to her, "I who speak to you am He." (John 4:26)

With these words, everything changed. A floodlight of truth illuminated her mind. By the way, this was the first time in Scripture when Jesus publicly and specifically declares himself to be "the Christ." And note that this monumental and historic revelation wasn't made to the Pharisees or Jewish leaders. It wasn't even made at a religious gathering. Not announced on the Sabbath, it instead occurred at the end of a long ordinary day's journey. He didn't choose to reveal Himself in Jerusalem, but rather in a relatively obscure little town. He made this statement not in the temple, but at the city watering hole. He shared this monumental truth with a woman, not a man. With a Samaritan, not a Jew. In a conversation, not a sermon.

But what He said was even more significant than where, how, and to whom He said it. Literally, Jesus declared to her, "I AM." Because the Samaritans believed the first five books of Moses, she would have likely been familiar with the story in Exodus 3:14 where God reveals Himself to Moses at the burning bush. Asked His name, God simply replied, "I AM THAT I AM" is My Name. Those two English words "I AM" are just one word in the original Hebrew—the word Yahweh. It's the most personal, intimate, true and revealing Name of God. It's the name He calls Himself. Jesus could have told her many things that day, but He chose to let her know He was the great "I AM."[96]

## Well, WELL!

Now, how would you feel if you suddenly discovered the man who had asked to borrow a dollar at the drink machine turned out to be God Almighty in human flesh? Would your mouth go bone dry? Possibly feel a chill gallop like a wild stallion up your spine? Maybe grow a little weak in the knees? *Drop* to your knees? Perhaps feel a bit embarrassed because you had been treating Him like an ordinary person? What would you do? Call a friend? Call 911? And what would you have said to Jesus? As for this woman, we will never know what was about to come out of her mouth because at that very moment, the disciples showed up with dinner. They no doubt marveled upon discovering Jesus talking to the woman. But He was the Teacher, and the Man in charge, so nobody said anything to Him about it. Meanwhile, the Samaritan woman hastily made her exit upon seeing a group of Jewish males approaching. So she hurriedly leaves Jesus, the well, and her water pot. She had gone to the well to get some cool water, but in reality, the Well had come to her! And He filled her up so much that she began overflowing with living water. Jesus saw her as a person with great "worship potential." She was ripe for a spiritual harvest. The timing was perfect, and so was Jesus' approach. The Lord never did get that drink from her, but she sure got one from Him. Can you see her now? Eyes brimming with tears of joy and excitement, racing back into town that evening? She immediately runs to tell "the men"—most likely her former husbands and lovers—about this wonderful Stranger she had met.

> A God as great as ours will always have true worshipers! Even in the Tribulation. That's how worthy He is.

"Come, see a man who told me all the things that I have done; this is not the Christ, is it?" (John 4:29)

More accurately translated, this phrase reads, "Is this not the Christ?" as she is clearly proclaiming, "It's Him!"

And they listened to her as others also began coming out to Him (John 4:30). Meanwhile, the disciples were trying to get Jesus to eat something. But He wasn't hungry anymore.

"I have food to eat that you do not know about. The disciples, therefore, were saying to one another, 'No one brought Him anything to eat, did he?' Jesus said to them, 'My food is to do the will of Him who sent Me, and to accomplish His work.'" (John 4:32–34)

Jesus is essentially telling them, "There is something more satisfying and fulfilling to Me than a hot meal after a long day's journey. Something even more thirst quenching than a cold cup of this well water. You need to know that My greatest desire is to seek lost people and turn them into true, spiritual worshipers of God. Look around you! There are potential worshipers all over this place! Think of how much glory the Father can receive through these people! That's what motivates Me. That's what occupies my mind. Not food."

> You need to know that My greatest desire is to seek lost people and turn them into true, spiritual worshipers of God. Look around you! There are potential worshipers all over this place!

It is almost certain this woman became a worshiper of God that day. But not just any ordinary, average, common worshiper. Not the "Sunday only" kind. She became one who had learned to worship in "spirit and truth." She was exactly who Jesus was searching for. She was the reason He *had* to pass through Samaria. It was for *her*. Don't you love the way Jesus meets us as individuals. So personal. She was so enslaved to her sin that not even a husband's love could save her. She didn't need one more person looting her emotions and stealing what little she had left in the wreckage of her so-called "life." It was going to be just another day on the bottom of the ocean for her. But when Jesus dropped anchor that day, her world was injected with a full and healthy dose of heavenly hope. He did way more than just locate her. He dove down to the bottom and met her where she was, right there at the same well she visited every day of her dull existence. He spoke her language, revealing the whole truth to her. But He did something even better than that. He raised her wreckage to the surface. Then, in a way only a real Messiah could do, He completely restored her. He made her life "seaworthy." And worth living. He gave her salvation, a future and real hope. Then Jesus charted a whole new course for her. The past was officially the past. Her life was re-christened and she discovered for the first time that she was not beyond the reach of grace, love, and the heart of God.

And as a result of becoming a true worshiper of Christ, "from that city many of the Samaritans believed in Him because of the word of the woman who testified." (John 4:39)

Beautiful.

That's what can happen when the world encounters the real thing.

God is looking for true worshipers.

Are you one?

# Endnotes

1. Adam, with his enhanced mental capacity, had already accomplished the incredible feat of naming all the cattle, birds, and beasts of the field (Genesis 1:20).
2. Prior to Noah's Flood, some creation scientists believe the sun's harmful ultraviolet rays were filtered out by a water-filled canopy covering the entire earth. This could also account for why people lived for hundreds of years.
3. 2 Corinthians 11:14
4. Ezekiel 28:13–15; Isaiah 14:12–14; Luke 10:18; Revelation 12:8–10
5. Job 38:4–7; Genesis 3:1–3
6. The Hebrew word for "serpent" used in Genesis 3:1 is *nachash*, and some scholars believe the word originally referred to a creature that walked upright. See Henry Morris, The Genesis Record (Baker Book House, 1976), p.108.
7. The Bible nowhere states the serpent was in a tree. On the contrary, it is described as a "beast of the field," and compared to cattle in this respect (Genesis 3:14). Though there is no conclusive evidence to prove either portrayal (whether in a tree or on the ground), there is every indication that it went from having legs to being forced to slither on the ground like present-day snakes (Genesis 3:14).
8. Hebrews 11:25
9. Ephesians 2:1–3,5; Colossians 2:13
10. Jeremiah 17:9
11. Ecclesiastes 1:1–3, 2:10–11, 2:25, 3:11–13, 12:1–4
12. John 6:44, 65; Romans 3:10–12; Ephesians 2:1–2; Jeremiah 17:9; 1 Corinthians 2:14
13. Augustine, (Book 1)
14. See also Romans 11:33–36
15. Notice in Genesis 3:9 that God calls out to the man first, not the woman who had first sinned by eating the fruit. This is because man was created initially and given the task of governing creation and leading and protect-

ing his wife (Genesis 2:19–20; 1 Corinthians 11:3; Ephesians 5:23; Colossians 3:18). Adam was likely with Eve when she took the fruit. He was not innocent, but rather complicit and ultimately responsible for the fall. That's why Romans 5:12–21 states it was through *Adam's* disobedience that sin entered the human race, cursing and condemning it.

16. Other examples of Christophanies include: Genesis 31:11, 13; Exodus 3:2, 4; Judges 6:11–14; 13:3–23.
17. Genesis 18:25; Deuteronomy 32:4
18. See Revelation 12:7–12
19. Genesis 2:15–16
20. It is not entirely clear as to when Adam and Eve were actually saved. The Bible never explicitly states that they were saved at this time, though it is often assumed. However, Eve does acknowledge God at the birth of her 3rd son, Seth. It was after Seth's son, Enosh was born that humanity began to call on the name of the Lord (Genesis 4:25). Because God pursued Adam and Eve, found them, clothed them, and then protected them is indication that they had been redeemed by Him.
21. It is not known how long the Garden lasted or was visible to men, but should any part of it remained until Noah's day, it surely was wiped away in the flood.
22. https://bible.org/question/does-ielohimi-gen-11-mean-god-or-gods
23. Moses uses the same word ('corrupt') to describe both Noah's generation in Genesis 6:11 and the people of Israel in Exodus 32:7. Also, the phrase "rose up to play" utilizes the same word later used to portray the sexual caressing between a man and a woman (cf. Exodus 32:6; Genesis 26:8).
24. Actually, with this sin, they violated the first three of the Ten Commandments (see Exodus 20:3–7).
25. Psalm 115:3
26. For a more extensive discussion concerning God, evil, and suffering, see Jeff Kinley, *Uncovering the Mysteries of God* (Regel)
27. Deuteronomy 10:14; Psalm 50:10, 24:1
28. Revelation 19:11–21; 20:11–15
29. Genesis 37:20–28, 50:20
30. John 3:36
31. Lamentations 3:22; Romans 5:8–9; 6:23; Ephesians 2:8–9
32. Romans 8:1
33. Paul also said he wished those false teachers would go "mutilate themselves." Harsh language, but in the theological context of Paul's argument, it actually was a "reasonable" response, considering that they were requiring believers to be circumcised as a necessary "add on" to salvation

by faith. "Since you want believers to cut themselves to prove their salvation, why don't you guys just go ahead and go all the way and castrate yourselves!" (see Galatians 5:12)

34. Romans 6:23
35. Matthew 15:9, NIV
36. For a more in-depth study on the sin nature – what it is, how it operates, and how to overcome it, see Jeff Kinley, *The Christian Zombie Killers Handbook* – Slaying the Living Dead Within (Thomas Nelson, 2011)
37. 2 Peter 3:18
38. Hebrews 12:4ff
39. 2 Samuel 6:21–23
40. Luke 5:28
41. Matthew 11:19
42. Matthew 12:31–37
43. Matthew 9:12–13
44. Ibid. Paraphrased.
45. 1 King 17:9
46. See also Matthew 8:10, 15:28
47. Mark 7:25–26
48. Matthew 15:23
49. Matthew 11:28–30
50. cf. Matthew 7:7
51. Isaiah 55:8–9
52. Matthew 15:24; Mark 7:27; Acts 3:26; Romans 1:16
53. Job 13:15
54. Mark 1:45; 6:33; Luke 8:4, 19, 19:3
55. Matthew 14:8
56. Matthew 14:21
57. Matthew 14:15
58. John 14:3; 17:24; Philippians 1:23; 1 Thessalonians 4:17; Revelation 3:20–21, 17:14, 20:4
59. Mark 14:3
60. Luke 9:54
61. Acts 12:2
62. Psalm 63:3; Hebrews 13:5
63. Mark 14:3–5
64. Mark 14:3; John 12:3

## Endnotes

65. Mark 14:4–5
66. John 12:6
67. Revelation 2:5
68. Romans 8:16
69. Isaiah 37:33–35
70. Isaiah 37:36
71. Isaiah 37:35–38
72. 1 Kings 18:27
73. Compare 2 Kings 1:9–14
74. Revelation 6:12–17, 16:9, 11, 21
75. Revelation 1:7
76. Matthew 16:4
77. John 6:15, 18:36
78. Matthew 13:1–2; Mark 4:1–34
79. Job 36:32, 38:1–41
80. Luke 8:25
81. Mark 5:1–20
82. See Psalm 46
83. Matthew 28:20; Hebrews 13:5
84. Isaiah 55:8–9
85. Romans 3:10–12
86. Luke 19:10; John 6:44, 65, 12:32; Ephesians 2:1–2
87. Jeremiah 5:1
88. Warren Weirsbe, *Be Alive* (Colorado Springs, David C. Cook Publishing, 1986), 64.
89. See Matthew 10:5. Jesus did this because His primary mission was first to the Jewish people.
90. 1 John 4:8
91. Author's paraphrase of John 4:21–22
92. Acts 7:48, 17:24
93. Isaiah 29:13; Matthew 15:8
94. 2 Timothy 3:16–17; 2 Peter 1:3
95. Philippians 3:10
96. Later Jesus would say the same thing to the same Jews who accused Him of being a demon-possessed Samaritan. Their response was to attempt to stone Him for blasphemy and making Himself out to be equal to the Father. See John 8:42–59

www.ingramcontent.com/pod-product-compliance
Lightning Source LLC
Chambersburg PA
CBHW060532100426
42743CB00009B/1507